Asante Sana
TANZANIA

Jackal

Asante Sana TANZANIA

Martin and Donna's Safari to Tanzania
October 8 to October 26, 2012

Our journal recordings, accountings, and various tidbits along the way!

By Donna Marie Seim

Peter E. Randall Publisher
Portsmouth, New Hampshire
2016

Printed in the U.S.A.

ISBN: 978-1-937721-27-5

Library of Congress Control Number: 2015956492

Nonfiction, Safari travel, Tanzania, Zanzibar, African cultures and wildlife, Maasai

Published by Peter E. Randall Publisher
Portsmouth, New Hampshire 03802
www.perpublisher.com

Book design by Grace Peirce

DEDICATION

Asante Sana, Tanzania is dedicated to my husband, Martin, the man behind the lens! His photography of these beautiful images became the inspiration to rewrite our journal notes creating *Asante Sana, Tanzania.*

I would like to thank my Pen Friends for their constant moral support of my writing and helping me with MONKEY DRAMA! And my pen friend, Suzanne DeWitt Hall, who edited my rough draft and urged me to tell more, more and more!

Thank you to Zakariah Johnson, from Peter E. Randall Publisher, for his superb editing and keeping me consistent and my snakes straight!

Thank you to Grace Peirce for her superior graphic skills and her creative photographic placement.

Thank you to Deidre Randall, from Peter E. Randall Publisher, for turning my manuscript into this handsome coffee-table book, *Asante Sana, Tanzania.*

Lappet-faced Nubian vulture

Contents

The To-do Checklist!

For decades, a safari in Africa had been a dream for us. Once Martin made the deciding ultimatum, that it was indeed time for us to go to Africa, our lengthy preparations began! We started with the required research and sent for all the catalogs from every safari company we could find. Each company presented their safaris as exciting, adventurous, and oh-so-very Hemingway! After much deliberation, we chose Thomson Safaris because they went to Tanzania only. We reasoned that if they specialized in safaris in Tanzania for thirty years, they should be the most knowledgeable about the country we chose. We liked the fact that their headquarters were Boston-based, they proved to be a delight to talk to on the phone, and the tents looked as inviting as any tent could possibly be.

Once we signed up and confirmed our safari dates with the Thomson crew, the wheels of motion began to churn. The first thing they sent us was *the* to-do checklist, which comes along with *the* safari bible of handy things to know and plan for on your first real safari to Africa. Number one on the list was to apply for visas from the Tanzanian embassy. It sounds straightforward; but in order to receive our visas, we had to mail them our actual passports. That made us nervous; but after a couple of weeks, they came back along with our visas. Check!

Martin booked our flights with Delta and KLM. Thomson did the rest of the booking for our entire trip. That was easy! Check.

Next, we made appointments for our shots. Our visit with the infectious disease doctor was slated for mid-morning. After chatting with the doctor, who took copious notes about the destinations of our intended travel and our medical histories, he disappeared, and the nurse, armed with needles, arrived on the scene. She cheerfully dispensed five shots into Martin's arms and four into mine. Tetanus (just in case), flu (might as well), whooping cough (including random other diseases), and hepatitis—both kinds—to be extra safe in case we happened to be around someone else's blood. Typhoid and a polio booster because polio still exists in Tanzania. Oops! Nurse apologizes profusely; there is only enough typhoid for one so I have to come back for mine. Then we got the good news: there is no yellow fever in Tanzania, yay! Check!

That evening at five o'clock I felt myself sinking into a pool of pain. My arms felt like lead weights; I realized I could not lift them higher than a thirty-five-degree angle from my body. My upper arms felt as if a long-horned mountain goat had rammed them. After three days and no improvement, I called the nurse and whined, "My arms are still sore!"

"Do you have a fever or a rash?"

"No, just my arms hurt."

"Oh, then you are fine. Take some Advil." So I did. It took a whole week for me to regain normalcy. Martin bounced back in a day! Meanwhile, I still had to go back and get my typhoid shot. I was not looking forward to that! We also had one more hepatitis shot to go before we left, then one more little jab three months after we returned home. At this point I felt invulnerable; I could not possibly contract any kind of disease. I was ready for anything, except, of course, bacteria; so as recommended, we brought along two prescriptions of Cipro, an antibiotic, to be taken at the first sign of intestinal distress. Check!

We had discovered that there were two potential types of malaria pills. One of these can cause horrible nightmares; this would be the last thing we would want to experience anywhere, especially while camping out with wild animals. We chose the kind that did not cause nightmares. Check!

I packed the equivalent of a full medicine cabinet of supplies! Nurse Donna at the ready. Check! The safari bible recommended bringing along a set of eyebrow tweezers, so I made sure I had a good sturdy pair, not wanting to think about what I might need to pluck out besides gone-astray eyebrows. Check!

Next was my search for a hat with a wide brim. I sent away for a nice woven garden hat from a catalog. The brim was too big, I looked like I was playing dress up, and the strings tying under my chin would drive me crazy.

I moved on to the official online safari store and bought a funky safari hat with folding brim. Check! Bought two duffel bags. Check! Bought lightweight day backpack. Check! Bought wick-away socks. Check! Bought biodegradable soap and shampoo. Check! Bought lightweight washcloths. Check! Bought antiseptic hand wipes. Check! Bought toothbrush sanitizers. Check! Purchased safari shirt, long-sleeved. Check! Purchased safari pants, with zippers and secret pockets. Check! Purchased knee-length safari shorts. Check! Purchased nylon rain jacket, lightweight, with hood. Check! Purchased two flashlights and headlamps. Check! Purchased zebra-striped and cheetah-spotted kerchiefs for dust protection. Check! Purchased money belt for Martin and money purse for me. Check! Purchased short-sleeved cotton jersey and long-sleeved cotton jersey. Check! Purchased sunglasses, two kinds. Check! Search for curlers, the spongy kind to set hair with when enduring no electricity. Ugh. Check! Purchased converter and plug outlets for electric hair curler when able to secure electricity. Check!

Martin bought a new camera and camera memory cards. He bought all his safari clothes from a farm catalog. Check!

By this time our bedroom looked like an outdoor-adventure shop. Martin and I were counting down the days! Only two weeks to go until takeoff.

Time to organize our travel money, the paper kind, for tips, drinks, and treasures to bring home. I made a trip to our local bank and asked for ones, fives, tens, twenties, fifties, and some hundreds. I assured the teller that I was traveling to a third world country and not going to a casino in Las Vegas. The teller counted it and put it in an envelope. The next trick was to stuff it in small batches in moneybags and belts. Oops, I reread safari bible; it states that they, the Tanzanians, want bills after the year 2000 with no marks or tears. The cleaner the bills, the better, and not folded; the why of this was not explained but I believed the book. I sent Martin back to the bank to get new clean, unmarked, unfolded bills. He tried our regular bank and then two other banks but, nope, no new bills to be had, only at Christmas. Back to our bank, the teller worked with Martin and found the best bills she had. We now had a pile of okay bills, not crisp and new, but not torn or worn. Check!

I couldn't help wondering whether a porter or a waiter or a trinket seller would truly hand our money back to us and say, "This will never do!" in Swahili?

At last it was time to pack. We were allowed one duffle and one backpack each. Each duffle and its contents could not weigh more than thirty-three pounds. We kept strictly to the list of what we would need but still felt that we would weigh in at more than thirty-three pounds. We held our breath and weighed ourselves; then we weighed ourselves with our duffle. A miracle, Martin's duffle weighed in at twenty-nine pounds and mine was thirty-one pounds. Whew. Check!

Takeoff Day!

Monday, October 8

Monday, October 8, finally came. Our duffels were packed, repacked, and reweighed for the last time. Kristin, our daughter, picked us up and drove us to Boston's Logan Airport. Next stop, Amsterdam!

Due to flight times, we knew we would be spending the night in Amsterdam, so we had pre-booked a hotel room in the Amsterdam airport. That worked out well, allowing us to catch up on lost sleep and helping to diminish the fatigue of jet lag. We found the Amsterdam airport to be delightful. There, you could shop in a modern, upscale, underground mall, enjoy a cup of tea, and nibble a sandwich sitting in a giant delft teacup! We had saved our frequent flyer points so we could fly business class. We flew KLM airlines and were treated like royalty the entire flight to Mount Kilimanjaro Airport. After an eight-hour flight, however, we were quite happy to have landed in Tanzania!

Tanzania

Wednesday, October 10

Once we deplaned and located our duffle bags, we looked for other matching Thomson Safaris duffle tags and hats. To our great pleasure, we spotted a big group of charming, intelligent looking people surrounding a fellow holding up a Thomson Safaris sign. Hooray, this must be our group! As we approached the group, another young man came rushing up behind us waving a Thomson Safaris sign. He asked our names and, after we told him, said, "Come with me." We followed him like puppy dogs, feeling bewildered, because we were the only ones being led to his Thomson van. He deposited our duffle bags in the rear of the van and we hopped inside. Still confused, I asked if there were others coming with us.

"No, it's just you two."

"What about the group over there getting into the other vans?"

"Oh, they are going on a safari!"

"But, so are we! Aren't we going on the same safari?"

"No, they are going on another safari, different from yours."

Without another word of explanation, he hit the gas pedal and the van careened out of the airport parking lot and proceeded to speed down the road, disappearing into the ink-black night. Martin and I looked wide-eyed at each other, both of us wondering if we were possibly being kidnapped. We asked his name and he answered, "Simon." He was clearly not the chatty type. The van flew down the road, farther and farther from the airport and any signs of civilization.

Finally, after over an hour, which felt like an eternity, he pulled into a dirt drive with a sign reading "River Trees Inn." This move was very encouraging because River Trees Inn was the first stop on our itinerary. Relieved, we jumped out of the van. The gentleman from the inn joined us outside and gestured for us to sit on a wooden bench; he then proceeded with a very formal registration, asking for all our information and to see our passports. I felt as if we were guilty until proven innocent, possible smugglers sneaking over the border? Once the paperwork was completed, the porter, who had been waiting patiently, graciously led us our room. As we scurried after the porter, Simon

Donna at Arusha Airport

called after us that he would be back at six-thirty the next morning to take us to Arusha airport. We waved in agreement as he disappeared into the night. It was dark and near impossible to see where we were going. With careful footing, we traversed the winding path that led to a separate cottage. Despite our efforts at sleep in Amsterdam, we were definitely jet lagged and sleep hungry. The room was lovely, and I tried to absorb the essence of our first experience in an African inn. But weary from travel, we showered and climbed into the mosquito-netted bed.

At two-thirty in the morning we were woken by Martin's phone buzzing with a message from the phone company telling us we were out of range. Didn't we rent this special international phone so we would be covered in Africa? After the rude cell phone wake up, we had our first experience negotiating the layers of mosquito netting, which required considerable calisthenics, especially when we were in a hurry to get to the bathroom! Martin's feet landed outside the netting, but his head was caught somewhere in between. I giggled at Martin being stuck as I unwrapped the covers and then slid my toes out to the floor, lifting the netting up over my head as I went. After a successful round trip to the bathroom, we fell into a deep slumber until the alarm went off at five-thirty a.m.

The winding trail to the dining room was barely visible because it was still black as night outside. Breakfast was delicious: the cooks were eager to bestow us with a feast of fruits, juices, tea or coffee, scrambled eggs, and sausage or ham, followed by round, crunchy rolls dripping with butter and jam. But, unfortunately, we needed to eat fast! Simon had arrived and was waiting for us by the door, jangling his keys!

ARUSHA

Thursday, October 11

We eagerly hopped into Simon's van. We were ready for our first sightings of Africa in daylight! Our destination was the city of Arusha, the central hub for this area of Tanzania. The road was peppered with school-age children lining the sides of the streets. One group was dressed in green school uniforms; another group was dressed in blue. Some of the children carried little brooms while others had sticks. I wondered if it had anything to do with wild animals. I asked, and Simon said the children brought the hand-woven brooms to school to take turns cleaning the yard. The children glanced our way with mild curiosity as they marched on. Women walked by, balancing baskets on their heads. Small shops with opened fronts lined the street. People walked and talked, some were busy burning small fires of what looked like trash by the side of the road.

As we got closer to the center of Arusha the bustling intensified. My eyes were darting from one side of the road to the other. Oxen carts laden with produce lined the road. Simon, now talkative and acting as an official guide, pointed out all the points of interest: the Lutheran church, the university, the courthouse, the bank, and on and on. As we rounded a corner we watched two young boys push a wooden cart, full to the brim with tomatoes, up a very steep road. Cars and motorbikes zoomed around them. Following the boys and their tomato cart, we came upon the marketplace. Teeming would be too calm a word to describe this scene; rather, it was frenzied. The universal language was understood: from the body posturing, hand gesturing, and facial expressions; the ancient art of bargaining and haggling was taking place. Colorful fabrics of Maasai tribal clothes combined with a bright patchwork of produce awakened my artistic sense like candy to a child. I wanted the van to halt; I wanted to breathe the smells and make the marketplace mine. Simon, who had no intention of stopping, informed us that this was the major and only marketplace, not just for Arusha, but also for the entire surrounding countryside for many, many miles.

Simon had a schedule to adhere to and he made sure we were at the airport on time. The airport turned out to be nothing more than a small puddle-jumper garage. Once there, we realized we didn't have our tickets, or know the name of our actual destination. All we knew was that we were going to a Thomson camp, the eastern one, on the Serengeti. Simon told us to sit down in the small waiting area. He then busied himself talking to the man behind the desk. He conducted the entire transaction for us and brought us our boarding passes. We said a quick goodbye and Martin handed him the first of our never-ending stream of tips. I had to laugh. Martin, the rebel, folded the money before he gave it to Simon. He did so for all tips he handed out the entire trip!

Sitting next to us in the waiting area was a nice young couple on safari, but we soon found out they were not with Thomson. Another group of people gathered near us waiting for their flight. We began chatting with them and when they headed off as a group toward their plane we followed along. We felt like sheep, but at this point that felt good. One gentleman noticed that our boarding passes looked different than theirs, but we didn't worry about it, because nothing seemed particularly normal. Just as we were approaching the aircraft, a man came running after us frantically waving his arms. "No! Wait! Don't get on that plane! That is not your plane! You are going to Lobo! You are going on this plane." His outstretched arms waved our eyes towards a tiny propeller plane, much smaller than the one we had been heading for!

So, now we knew, we were going to Lobo, which we later found out was located in Tanzania very near the border of Kenya. What we didn't know was how long it was going to take us to get there!

We climbed the short ladder to the body of the propeller plane and took our seats behind the nice young couple we had met earlier. The four of us were the only passengers. We already knew they were not on a Thomson safari; so, we wondered, why were they on the same plane? The pilot introduced himself. He told us he was the son of Australian missionaries; he was brought to Africa as a little boy and grew up in Africa, never returning to Australia. He loved Africa. He then informed us that we would fly the first couple to their camp, a short twenty-minute run.

It was a smooth flight. Clouds of white fluff floated by, the twenty minutes ticked past quickly, and soon the

Our Puddle Jumper!

ground grew closer as we began our decent. My eyes opened wide as I sucked in a deep breath, plastering my forehead against the windowpane to witness our first sight of zebra! The zebras were walking in an absolute straight line, head-to-tail and tail-to-head. I couldn't count them there were so many!

"Look! I can see round, wet hippos cavorting right there in the small river down below. This is so incredible!" I felt my first rush of being so close to wild animals.

Then we both spotted hundreds of wildebeests standing on the very landing strip where we were about to land. "Wildebeests!"

The pilot, acting not troubled in the least, shouted back at us, "Don't worry; I'll fly over them and make a short landing." I anxiously thought, here goes, a wild wildebeest landing! But as we approached, the wildebeests scattered, kicking their hooves in every direction. As if on command, they parted directly in the middle of the airstrip, giving us plenty of landing room. An exciting beginning to our safari!

We hopped out of the plane, eager to stand on African soil. The other couple's driver and van were there, so we waved goodbye, calling out after them, "*Kwaheri*" (Goodbye).

Martin informed the pilot he needed a quick tire check and the pilot nodded to him. The pilot and I chatted amiably, standing safely next to the doorway of the plane. Suddenly an alarmed look crossed his face, "Where is your husband?"

"Oh, he is off in the bush. He'll be right back."

"I thought he meant a tire check right here! Call him back! Quick!"

I yelled to Martin, who was about thirty yards into the bush. "Mart, the pilot wants you back." My heart was pounding like the hooves of the wildebeests!

"Okay, coming."

The pilot was beside himself. Martin, with a very red face, scurried back to the plane. The pilot spoke to him as if he were a schoolboy, "There could have been a lion out there! Never, ever, go into the bush alone!"

Okay, we were learning fast—this is for real!

Once we got back into the plane and attached our seat and shoulder belts, the pilot announced we were going to another spot to pick up a group that had just finished up their safari. It would take us about one hour and fifteen minutes. I gulped, over an hour in the small plane and it wasn't our final destination. I decided to read the magazine in the seat pocket in front of me from cover to cover including the small print. The flight itself was smooth, so I began to relax to a point. And then, I looked up from the magazine. The pilot's attention was completely focused on filling out paperwork! My tummy lurched. Shouldn't he have his hands on the controls and his eyes scanning the sky? Did I mention that there was no copilot?

Eventually, I felt the plane begin to descend. I was

relieved that the ride was almost over. When suddenly the plane tipped sideways, our wings zapped into a ninety-degree plunge. I let out a terrified *WHOOP* and jammed my knees tight against the seat in front of me, grabbing onto Martin's arm at the same time. Within a few microseconds, we straightened out to a horizontal position. The pilot apologized profusely, "Sorry, marabou stork. They are the stupidest birds ever; they never get out of your way! They have a wingspan of eight feet. Huge dumb birds! Had to swerve to miss him, or we would have gone down. I really am sorry; I didn't mean to frighten you!" (This was all delivered in a drawling Australian accent!)

Thompson gazelle

"That's okay, I'm fine. It was just a sudden surprise, that's all." Panting and suffering from dry mouth, I gulped a swish of lukewarm water from my near-empty water bottle. At this point I was really ready to strangle the pilot. Martin, usually calm in puddle jumpers, was sitting upright and alert.

Shortly we were on the ground once again, but this time we didn't have time to get out and stretch our legs. Eight passengers climbed in and soon we were airborne. The pilot called out, "Next stop, Lobo, a twenty-minute ride." We had left Arusha airport before nine a.m. and we would be flying into Lobo well after eleven o'clock. So much for a short airplane ride!

Finally, our destination, Lobo! We deplaned. There, waiting for us, was our guide, Kileo. His eyes smiled warmly as he reached out to shake our hands. He stood tall, a mature African man with a touch of gray in his hair and kind brown eyes. I felt comfortable with him immediately. We were soon to learn that he was an expert on African wildlife and his special love was birds.

I asked if we were the only ones he was picking up. He replied, "Yes, just you two."

"Are there more people at the camp?" I asked, hoping they came early for some reason or another.

"No, you are the only ones staying at the camp tonight. But there will be others in a day or so." He grinned widely, the second of many Kilco smiles.

"Let's get going now; we have lots of road to cover before we make it to the eastern camp." He seemed relaxed and friendly, so we headed off in our latest conveyance, a Range Rover. It didn't take long before we were spotting animals left and right. Kileo said we had brought the luck with us. It was thrilling; we were really in Africa and on safari! Striped zebras (*punda millia*) were everywhere; giraffes (*twigga*) with long lovely necks paraded by us with loping steps as only a giraffe could do. Warthogs rolled in muddy puddles along the road, and upon hearing our approach, ran off with tails straight up in the air with their babies following in suit. Elephants (*tembo*) rumbled straight out of a forest to find a water hole; wildebeests gathered, snorting in large herds; tons and tons of Thompson gazelles (tommies) darted playfully with non-stop tail wagging. Our eyes were blurred with the sightings and our stomachs were beginning to rumble. Breakfast was eons ago and the sun was getting way past the yardarm. I hoped we would make camp before too long. Apparently Kileo had been indulging us in our sightseeing because he said, "Okay, you have seen plenty; there are more of these everywhere. Now we must get to camp." And so we did, bump after bump at the highest speed the Range Rover would allow. My first Serengeti massage!

Ahh, Camp!

We were ceremoniously greeted by the staff who were lined up and standing at attention. They all wore the same uniform of blue jeans and green Thomson T-shirts. After many "*Jambo, jambos*" (Hello, hellos) from our greeters, we were given cool wet cloths to wash our hands and faces. A drink of passion fruit was delivered on a large tray to quench our thirst and wash down the dust in our throats.

One staff member, Ishmail, who seemed to be assigned to us, brought us to our tent. I noted that our tent was handily located next to the main dining tent. Bathroom rituals needed special explanation; Ishmail demonstrated how to flush our toilet and manage the lever for a shower. We were informed

Tembo (elephant)

Martin looking very Hemingway!

Kileo

that we would need to request ahead for shower water to be brought to our tent. The water would be brought in a big drum; it would then be poured into a bucket outside the tent. When given the signal, the person inside the shower stall pulls the lever, and bingo—water drizzles out a nozzle over your head. The trick is to get wet all over as quickly as possible, then snap the lever up, slather soap all over yourself, and finally pull the lever to rinse. Water is precious in the Serengeti; all of it has to be driven in from Arusha, many miles away. After our convoluted plane ride I couldn't begin to judge the distance from our camp to anywhere!

To my dismay, I found that the flushing mechanism on our toilet was a difficult operation. I pulled a muscle getting it to flush. (Later on I learned it was just our toilet that was difficult to flush, the others worked perfectly well!) I requested a shower right away; I desperately needed to rinse off the travel dust and refresh. The water was delivered promptly. However, I found it mildly disconcerting that the staff (male) person waited patiently outside for me to finish up my shower. As he explained, he needed to reclaim the unused water in the bucket for the next person's shower. It was, nevertheless, most reassuring to know that the water was warm and we had both shower and toilet facilities right inside our tent!

Kileo met us back at the dining tent for a late but hot lunch. We chatted and ate the beef and rice stew hungrily! Martin, totally accommodated as a vegetarian throughout the trip, was presented with a veggie medley with rice, which he declared was scrumptious. Afterwards we checked the campsite out, at which time Kileo strictly informed us that we were never to leave camp without being accompanied by a Maasai guard. We readily promised, remembering the pilot's warning about lion. The camp sat high on a ridge; the view down to the plain and the surrounding hills was stunning. Looking out from the porch of our tent we could see heads and necks of giraffes ambling by on the plain below. The birds sang and the wildebeests grunted non-stop as we settled into our comfy camp beds, falling into a traveler's slumber.

Our Maasai warrior

Feeling apprehensive, my forehead knitted into a knot as I asked, "Kileo, why only a bow and arrow?"

"Not to worry, Donna, the tips of the arrows are poisoned, so all he has to do is hit any part of the animal and it will die. I guarantee you he will not miss." I thought, that's fine, but I would really rather he carry a rifle with multiple bullets. I had spotted a camp guard sitting in front of the dining tent and he had a big shiny rifle! Maybe we could trade our Robin Hood in for a Maverick?

Before I could express any more concerns about arrows verses bullets, Ishmail began to lead us with great strides down the hill to the plain below, where wildebeests and giraffes were grazing.

We awoke late afternoon to bird song, and golden sunlight dappled through the screened windows of our tent. It felt dreamlike! We could tell the air was cooling down so we dressed in our safari gear—long pants, cotton shirts, light weight jackets, and walking shoes—and set out to find our guides. They were waiting for us along with Kileo. He introduced us once again to Ishmail, our guide from the camp who would soon be our *rafiki* (friend), along with our appointed Maasai warrior. The Maasai tribe is purported to be the fiercest in all of Africa. The warrior was dressed in plain khaki pants and jacket, not the colorful shawl-type robes that I had seen on Maasai in Arusha. He carried a simple bow and quiver of arrows. My concern was that we were going to walk on the expansive plain with more than one wild animal. If we should be attacked, how could one arrow save us from a pride of lions crouching hidden in the tall grass?

It was magnificent walking among the wildebeests. They were skittish; if we came too close they scurried away. The giraffes looked down at us with their giant eyes. At five feet two inches, I'm not exactly a tall person, but I never felt quite so small before. Their graceful movements were mesmerizing, and they, like the wildebeests, did not come too close, but watched us from a safe distance.

Over the crest of the plain, like a shimmering desert mirage, a Maasai woman, holding a baby and accompanied by a young boy and three donkeys, appeared on the horizon. Their stunning silhouettes were illuminated against the setting sun. We gasped in delight! Martin asked our warrior permission to take pictures and was given a very positive yes!

We finished our walk and arrived back at the camp just after the sun set. Kileo was waiting for us with sundowners set up on a portable table: beer for Martin

A walk on the wild side

Maasai and pundas (donkeys) on the horizon

and wine for me along with an assortment of crunchy snacks. (Sundowners are drinks to enjoy while watching the sunset. I believe this phrase was coined in Africa due to the spectacular sunsets.) A bonfire warmed us, shining bright against the darkening sky. After sharing stories about bird watching with Kileo, we were politely informed it was time for "washy, washy." A young man poured soapy water from a metal teakettle on our hands; with another kettle, holding clear water, he rinsed off the soap from our hands. This "washy, washy" became the absolute ritual before every meal. We were seated in the dining room, and once again we were keenly aware, and mildly disappointed, that we were the only guests. But the tent twinkled with candlelight and the attentive serving staff placed steaming bowls of soup in front of us. We were happy that Kileo stayed and dined with us. As we ate, he enthusiastically discussed the next day's agenda.

Later on we crawled into bed, tired and a little anxious about our first night sleeping in a tent. We listened to the rhythm of the wildebeests' snorts and grunts. They sounded like they were on our front porch,

Maasai mother and baby

Lilac-breasted roller

not on the plain far below. We learned that wildebeests don't sleep; at least not the ones on guard. They sing their snuffs, grunts, and muffs all night long. We were getting used to their noises when we both tensed upon hearing a *whooooooop whooooop* call from a nearby hyena. As I finally grew accustomed to the animal sounds, I felt the day's adventure melting into soft dreams, but that didn't last long because something snuffled along the edge of our tent, right near our heads! Thankfully, whatever it was, it didn't tarry for long, and as fatigue overcame fear, we slept soundly. *Lala salama!* (Sleep well!)

The next morning the glow of the rising sun lit up our canvas walls like a giant orange. Just outside our tent stood a tree filled with a choir of birds each singing their own glorious rendition of "Wake up, wake up, you sleepy head!"

Punda millia (zebra, or "striped donkey")

Maasai Boma and the Young Warriors

Friday, October 12

"*Jambo, jambo*!" was our wake up call, along with the welcomed delivery of a pitcher of warm water. After pulling on our slacks and shirts, we stepped outside to view the vista of wildebeests, zebras, giraffes, and antelope on the plain below us. It was a cool morning and partly cloudy.

We downed our chef-prepared breakfast of crepe-like pancakes drenched in syrup, sausage, fresh fruit, juice, and tea like we had never eaten before. We were then offered the second course of made-to-order eggs any way our hearts desired, along with ham or bacon. But our stomachs were already full and our spirits were high in anticipation of our first full day on safari. And Kileo was waiting patiently for us by the Range Rover. As we rushed towards him he greeted us with his winning smile and a, "*Habari?*" (How are you?)

We answered as he prompted us, "*Mzuri, asante sana*!" (I am well, thank you.) Our early morning tour consisted of meeting a vulture dining on his breakfast, an amazing termite hill as tall as me, numerous antelopes, the darling dik-dik (tiniest of the gazelles), tails-up warthogs, and a multitude of birds.

Kileo educated us on every bird we checked off on our bird sightings list. My favorite was the cinnamon-chested bee-eater. We also sighted birds of prey: the augur buzzard, the black-chested snake eagle, the kestrel and black-shouldered kite, the butler and tawny eagle; and of the bustard family we sighted both the kori bustard and the white-bellied bustard.

Throughout the trip we spotted many larger birds: crowned cranes, an Egyptian goose, flamingoes, guinea fowl, herons, and the fabulous African hoopoe, along with many hornbills and ibises.

The secretary bird, Martin's favorite, is known for killing snakes by pouncing on them with its clawed feet and then methodically jumping up and down, somewhat similar to a secretary banging on a keyboard!

As far as snakes go, Kileo warned us that the spitting cobra is one to be aware of! He informed us not to stick our heads inside any animal hole because a cobra might be lying there and if he spits, it is pure poison!

After a leisurely lunch back at the camp, we had the pleasure of meeting our cultural Maasai guide, Johnson Ketua Munge. He was tall and handsome in a red-checked cloak that wrapped around him like a shawl. He had the largest, most expressive eyes I have ever seen.

He gave us a briefing to school us on Maasai customs and manners before visiting a boma, the home of a Maasai family. He taught us to say *epa* (long e-pa) as we greeted the adults and that they would chant back to us *supa* (su-pa) or vice versa. Johnson did not tell us what the words translated to English meant, but it was the standard Maasai greeting. It didn't seem to matter which order the words were said as long as they were said. The children would wait respectfully until all the adults had been greeted and then they would come in a line and bow their heads. We were to touch the top of their heads and say *epa* after which they in turn would look up at us with respect and say *supa.*

Johnson, who had been to university in Arusha, spoke English well. He explained that the Maasai family was expecting us and we would be welcomed. We were instructed to bring flashlights because we would be invited to enter a home. He told us that it is so dark inside we would not be able to see without a light. We

Crowned Crane

Secretary Bird

also learned that there was no electricity in the boma and no running water.

He also informed us that the Maasai men take as many wives as they can afford. A man's bank account or wealth quotient is the number of cattle he owns. The more cows he owns, the more wives. All marriages are arranged between the father of the bride and the groom's father. Once the number of cows is agreed upon, the groom or the groom's family pays a dowry of cattle to the father of the bride. The number of cattle depends on the family; some brides are more expensive than others!

We were told that the women collect the firewood, carry the water from the well, mind the small animals, have babies, wash the clothes, and cook the meals. Men and older boys, until they become warriors at the age of seventeen, mind the cattle. The saying "a woman's work is never done" is a truism for the Maasai. After a wife has been married for several years and has had a number of children, she will say to her husband, "Husband it is time for a new wife!" The new and younger wife will share in the burden of the work and also the husband!

After our briefing, we drove to the nearby Maasai village, passing by a school where children were outside at recess. They were all Maasai, but not in their colorful traditional clothing. Instead, they wore uniforms making them look like the school children we had seen in Arusha. I wanted to stop and visit the school, but Johnson said we would return on Saturday.

Johnson Ketua Munge

The women shaved their heads

Kileo drove as far as he could into the bush following Johnson's directions; unfortunately, there was no visible road. The Range Rover is quite a machine, but it cannot go through dense bush. In exasperation, Kileo hit the brakes and said he would wait in the car. As we piled out of the Rover, Kileo gave us these words of warning, "Do not touch the dogs, they have rabies." I was shocked. I couldn't believe dogs belonging to the family could have rabies. Was this Kileo's way of expressing tribal rivalry?

Johnson led us a short distance through the bush to a compound of small huts surrounded by a thorny fence enclosure with a corral in the middle. Children peeked at us from behind one another. Several women approached us. They were dressed in sheets of bright red cloth, some with bold printed designs and some with checks. These were accompanied by other accent cloths in a spectrum of colors and tied together in handsome knots. The women all had shaved and beautifully shaped heads with long, stretched ear lobes laced with beads. Their slender necks were bedecked with cuffs and plates of elaborate beaded jewelry. Many of the women had babies tied to them, sling style. There were eight wives in all and one grandmother, whom we assumed was the mother of the husband. We greeted as we were taught, first the adults and then the children. I couldn't count how many children there were: newborn babies, boys of varying ages, and one adolescent girl. Some of the boys carried babies on their backs tied in slings. The boys did not look more than five or six years old, really still babies themselves. The children carrying children were not hindered in the least; they romped and played, and the babies bounced with them.

The children had flies in their eyes. It was especially difficult to watch the babies, who could not wave the pestering flies away because their arms and hands were restricted by the slings they were wrapped in. Some

Young Maasai boy carrying his sibling

of the children were sick; they had green goo running out of their noses right down to their lips. The cloths that covered them were dirty and torn. Their sandals consisted of simple leather soles with two crisscrossed straps to hold them onto their feet. As Martin took pictures of the children they gathered tightly round him, pressing in to see their own faces lit up on the camera screen. Smiling faces told us that they were delighted with their images! However, they were coughing, with deep, bad chest coughs and without hands to cover their mouths or rags or Kleenex to contain the germs.

The flies, which were everywhere, could be attributed to the animals. Baby goats were kept near the home until they became old enough to join the grazing herd. One of the boys picked up a black baby goat, carrying him around like a puppy. I yearned to pick one up too, until I noticed the diarrhea streaks down the back of his cute little goat legs. I was suddenly able to resist my impulse.

The dogs were plentiful and reminded me of the "potcakes" in the Caribbean. Africa is possibly where the name "potcake" came from because one of the dogs was licking what was on the bottom of a very battered pot. I wasn't worried about the dogs; they didn't look rabid. But I *did* think about how that pan was not going into a dishwasher with a sanitize button!

We learned from Johnson that each wife has her own house, her children living with her. Each structure was made of sturdy branches of bush woven together and cemented with cow dung and mud, topped with a thatched roof. The houses did not carry a trace of dung smell and Johnson told us that they were waterproof and extremely durable.

After greetings and picture taking, we were welcomed into one of the houses. Martin had to bow his head to pass through the doorway. The children surrounded us with enthusiasm and laughter, as if they were getting a special treat as well. I was stunned at the darkness inside. It was as dark as a moonless night. I thought my eyes would adjust, but no, it was impossible to make out what was inside without turning my flashlight on. I clicked it on. There was a small flicker of a fire on the floor, smoldering, with smoke filling the whole interior. Johnson pointed out the small slit in the roof that allowed a portion of the smoke to escape. My eyes watered from the smoke. Johnson pointed to an adjacent area with a blanket and a box. He told us the metal box was the family vault. The father always slept with it. There was another space for the children to sleep, a space so small they must curl up tightly together, which may be what keeps them warm at night. Our flashlights shone upon the last cubby in the room. Just beyond the fire sat a young woman breastfeeding a baby. Fearing we had invaded her privacy, we immediately shone our lights away from her. She did not stir. Johnson then pointed out a small fenced corral in the rear corner of the house. He explained that was where the baby goats would be put at night to protect them from wild animals. The larger stock of cows and goats would be rounded up at the end of the day and herded into the large circular corral inside the boma. The dogs were left outside of the corral to act as guards. Their barking or yelps would give the alert that a dangerous animal had entered the compound. That's when I understood that dogs were not pets!

Inside the boma

Once back outside, I asked Johnson, "Where is the water to drink and wash up with?" He explained that inside the house in a corner stood a black pot covered by a lid. That is where the drinking water is stored and kept cool. Fetching water is a never-ending chore. The women

Boys outside the boma (house)

Baby goat

carry the water from a well a distance away and back to the boma daily. As far as other water needs, I never saw a basin or sink of any kind, but clothes were draped and hung to dry on the branches of the bush outside the homes.

A baby bottle lay on the ground. It was made of a hollowed out gourd with a nipple on top. It was covered with flies.

Just then, through the willowy wood of acacia trees that surrounded the boma with needles as long as my fingers, we saw a flash of colors. There, before our eyes, was a stream of young warriors running and carrying raised spears as if in a deadly hunt. My breath caught in my throat at the awesome sight! Four older men brought up the tail of the group of twenty or so youths. Johnson explained that young Maasai men leave their families and live as a group in the wild from the age of seventeen to twenty-one to learn the ways of a warrior. During this time, they do not eat their meals with women. And, this is the only time they are allowed to grow their hair. In the old days, at the end of the four years they would be sent out alone to kill a lion and return bearing its heart. Having accomplished this task they would be held in high esteem as a warrior. It is now against the law to kill wild animals; at least in the Serengeti and national parks, so young warriors kill a cow instead and return with its heart. After they accomplish this final task the ritual is to shave off all the hair they have grown for four years. From this point on they are no longer young warriors but full-fledged Maasai warriors!

We had only a glimpse of the young warriors; they ran so fast and strong that Martin didn't even have time to point and shoot his movie camera. The vision, however, of the young warriors running silently through the trees has become a memory that will never leave me. Just as we were wishing we could get a closer glimpse of them; one, two, three young warriors circled back around into the boma. Apparently, they had spotted us, too!

They were magnificent. Their hair was braided or coiled in tight bands with elaborately designed hairpieces made of beads and metal, each one a unique expression of its wearer. One had four-inch beaded posts coming out of the back of his ear lobes; another had a metal sheath laced into his headpiece arcing almost two feet above his head. Their shawls sported bold colors of red, orange, and purple. They were adorned with layers of necklaces made with beads of many colors; they held their heads high and surveyed us with stern countenances.

Young warriors

Young warrior

The young warriors' expressions became less stern within a short time. They could not hold back from showing that they were extremely curious about Martin's camera, pointing to it with inquisitive gestures. Martin asked permission to take their pictures and they agreed, posing with great solemnity. Immediately after the picture taking they gathered around Martin to witness their images appearing on the camera screen. When the fiercest of the young warriors peered into the camera window, his eyes lit up in approval of his image and he thanked us with a huge ear-to-ear grin! This reinforced the fact that the one universal act of communication between all cultures and languages has to be the "smile." We couldn't help but smile back. These young warriors were just as enamored of themselves as teenagers in the Western world!

As this fun was wrapping up, the father of the family appeared quietly without offering the traditional greeting. He approached me reaching his hand out in the direction of my flashlight. I let him hold it and showed him how it worked. I had the feeling he wanted me to offer

Father of the family and Johnson

A lovely visit

it to him as a gift, but I only had one, and I knew I would need it as darkness enveloped the camp every evening. I gently retrieved it and was glad that he showed no ill will.

The women and children gathered in front of the boma's largest structure, which must have been their main house. The women talked and laughed with each other, obviously enjoying one another's company. The children played with the goats and one another, no toys, no bikes, no gadgets, just themselves, the land, and the animals. I wanted to take a seat on the dried patch of grass and join them; they were unhurried, and to me, seemed content with the moment and their lives and roles in it. I came away refusing to foist my North American values on them. The children may have had colds, and there were too many flies, but they had smiling eyes and beautiful faces!

As the sun began to sink lower in the sky, it was time to take our leave. I will never forget this one afternoon spent in a Maasai boma. "*Serena*, Maasai family! *Serena*." We waved and called out over and over again. They answered our calls and waves with, "*Serena, serena*!" (Goodbye, goodbye!)

Young Maasai girl

Serena, Goodbye

Eastern Serengeti Camp, the Uncooperative Cooperative

Saturday, October 13

The next day we took a seven a.m. walk before breakfast with Ishmail and our Maasai warrior, bow and arrows in hand. It was a cool morning, so we donned our warmest jackets and hats and headed down to the plain below us. The zebras were gone and it was pretty quiet until we spied, from a distance, three mongooses sitting upright in a row. As soon as they spotted us they disappeared, *zip,* down their hole. We circled the plain and headed back for camp. It was good exercise before a long day in the Range Rover, and now we were hungry and ready for breakfast. The first course was cereal and toast, with melon slices, juice, and tea or coffee. I placed my order, "*Chai, tafadhali. Asante sana.*" (Tea, please. Thank you very much.) Second course; eggs made to order, bacon, more fruit and cakes. Yummy! The chef is to be commended.

At ten a.m., we hopped into the Range Rover ready for our visit to the Tanzania Public School for the Maasai. Johnson had assured me that even though it was Saturday there would be children coming; he had made all the arrangements, spoken with the schoolmaster, etc. I was thrilled. I couldn't wait to see more Maasai children! I had brought my picture book *Where is Simon, Sandy*? to read to them. We planned that I would read in English and then Johnson would translate into Maasai, the children's mother tongue. Johnson explained that the Maasai speak their mother tongue at home and when they start school they will be taught Swahili, the national language of Tanzania. As they graduate to the higher grades they are required to study English.

Kileo stopped the Range Rover in the empty school lot. I glanced around with concern; it looked totally closed up, like a ghost town. Johnson said, "Stay here, I will find the schoolmaster."

A boy appeared out of nowhere, dressed in jeans and T-shirt. Kileo called to the lad and he approached the car. He was a good-looking boy with a winning smile. Kileo spoke to him in Swahili. He asked the boy about his exams. He hung his head and said he did not pass. Kileo was hard on him asking, "Why not?" He pointed out that he could not go on to the higher grades since he did not pass! The boy shook his head having no answer for Kileo. Kileo's tribe is known for being strong supporters of education. He expressed himself to us many times during our trip that he deeply felt the children would never get ahead in life if they were not educated. His sons and daughter were college educated with strong careers ahead of them. He was very proud of this.

At this point Johnson returned with a short man with an infectious smile. He greeted us, introducing himself as the headmaster of the school, and asked if we would like a tour. Becoming impatient I pouted, "We would love a tour but where are the children? I came to read my book to them."

The headmaster shrugged his shoulders, "Some came earlier in the morning, but you were not here. They did not want to wait because it was Saturday." Ugh! I was so disappointed; it was hard not to show it. I made Johnson promise me that he would return to the school and read my book to the children. He promised. Then, exasperated, we proceeded on our tour of the school. There was not much to see. There was one tiny room with a desk and schedules on the wall, some books in a pile, and a map of Africa. This was the headmaster's room. The next room beyond that was the library, very sparse for the number of children attending the school, which we were told was between 700 and 800 students. On our way out I noted that the class schedules were quite rigorous, beginning early in the morning and lasting until late afternoon. The subjects were varied and many, filling up all the hours of the day.

The tour continued to a classroom. The headmaster led us into the fairly large room; I was astounded that he would really show us this. It was a mess; there were papers torn and spread over and under desks. Books had toppled out from the meager shelf space under the desk onto the cluttered floor. It looked as if a dust devil had its way with the room, tearing it apart then leaving it in utter disarray.

We thanked the headmaster and gave him the books we had carried all away to Africa. We then said goodbye and departed. I felt cheated! I do hope Johnson kept his promise.

My picture book *Where is Simon, Sandy?* is the story of a little donkey that wouldn't quit, based on a true tale from the Caribbean. The beauty of reading it to the Maasai children was that they had their own donkeys, at least the luckiest of them did; the donkeys carried the water and the firewood on their saddles long distances to the boma. The donkeys saved the women from carrying it on their heads! I knew the children could relate to a story about a *punda* (donkey)!

The next stop on our agenda was the Women's Cooperative. It was a short, dusty, hot ride in the Range Rover. We were welcomed by bustling activity. The women of the co-op were lined up with their bright clothing and stunning white beadwork that shone bright against their black skin. As we approached they burst into song and dance. The dance consisted of a short hopping forward, causing the flat white plates of beadwork worn around their necks to flap up and down. The singing was loud and strong and high pitched, broken only by their laughter. One of the women, the most exuberant of the group, hopped ahead of the others. She seemed to be an elder of the group or maybe just plain old outgoing. After the dancing and singing we greeted them by shaking hands and saying *epa, supa, epa, supa*. They seemed pleased that we knew the custom.

The women retreated to a semi-circle of huts. In the center of the open circle there were long tables laden with gorgeous beadwork. We were greeted by Happiness—yes, that was her name—the organizer of the co-op, which was in its beginning stages. She was not Maasai but was from Tanzania. She told us she was an alumna of St. Olaf College in Minnesota. Martin's Alma Mater! She had returned to Tanzania to give back to her country. Martin was thrilled to meet another Olie in Tanzania! As you can imagine that led to a big hug and lots of shared memories!

It was time to shop for treasures to bring home. Martin went to one end of the tables and I to the other. The beadwork was exceptional. We met a woman in a batik print dress and matching headscarf whom Happiness brought into the co-op to teach the women how to make beaded items for tourists. I fell in love with the delicate beaded baskets and necklaces. Martin had his eye on the authentic pieces: the beaded plates and cuffs the women wore, a tube for carrying poison darts, and a beaded cross with silver colored dangles. It went on and on. We put our selections together, making quite a big pile. Only a few things had been priced, and the few prices labeled were in our opinion very moderate. We inquired how much we owed for our chosen treasures. Happiness quickly tallied up the selected pieces, and when she was done it came to just one hundred and fifty US dollars. Little did we know, at

The ladies of the Women's Cooperative

this point, that this experience was going to be a lesson in cultural misunderstandings and cooperative efforts in banking gone haywire!

Martin paid in cash and added a tip to contribute to the mission of the co-op, which was to help the women raise money for medical expenses. As she took the cash, Happiness explained to the women that the earnings would be kept in one bank account; when funds were needed it would be withdrawn to pay for medical costs. Happiness had earlier explained to us that far too many women die young for lack of medical care during pregnancies and birth. The money would also be used for health care needs for their children and husbands.

Unfortunately, the women either didn't approve

Understanding the cooperative concept

and I have tried to explain all the money goes into one pot to be shared. They don't get this concept, but they will!"

Martin took some photos and a short video of the confrontation. At one point, Happiness threw her arms in the air and walked away. She returned full force with more animated arguments, arms and voice raised, all for the cause of the co-op. It seemed reasonable that if people have never shared as a communal group, then shared savings for a rainy day must be a hard concept to swallow, even though it was intended for their medical welfare. Good luck, Happiness! (When we left, Happiness was not at all the epitome of her namesake.)

In the afternoon we had a private session with a Maasai storyteller. I recognized her immediately as one of the women from the co-op! I didn't detect any hard feelings from earlier in the day. With greetings of *epa* and *supa,* we settled in with Johnson as translator. One story was about her; she did not know her birthday or her age, but when she was young she was in love with a boy. When the time came for her to marry she was arranged to marry another. She was strong willed and did not want to marry this man. She cried and carried on but her father and mother would not listen. She was given cow's blood, cow's urine, and milk to drink. After

of the amount Happiness gave us as a price, or they simply didn't understand that they would not get paid for the individual pieces of work that they did. One young woman picked up a necklace I had purchased and spoke rapidly to Happiness. Happy answered, shaking her head, no, and speaking quite loudly back. A Maasai woman, who appeared to be the leader of the group, spoke her mind to Happiness in Maasai with a furrowed brow. Happiness defended her position without flinching. The teacher, who was brought in by Happiness, joined in the fevered debate. Martin and I backed off, telling Happiness we would be glad to pay more if they felt they were being cheated. "No, no. That is not it, they do not understand what a cooperative is,

Our storyteller

Common starling

drinking this mixture she lost all memory of her first love. She married the man they had chosen and she has lived a good life. She also told us the story about why the lion and hyena are enemies or how the hyena got his spots. After the stories, she sang us a song, and then we said, "*Serena!*"

A Wow Day!

Sunday, October 14

We woke to a symphony of birdsong from our nearby tree. Mourning and ring-necked doves, speckled mouse birds, lilac-breasted rollers, silver birds, flycatchers, common starlings with magnificent colors, yellow fronted canaries and lovebirds--all beckoned us to enter this new day in Africa! This was our last morning in our first camp, which had started to feel like home. Peeking out our tent flaps we saw sunshine and cool white clouds.

By now I had learned a bit of Swahili, and Ishmail was determined to instruct me every chance he had!

"*Jambo, jambo, habari*?" (Hello, hello, how are you?)

I responded, "*Jambo, jambo, Mzuri sana, asante sana*!" (Hello, hello, I am very well, thank you very much!)

"*Karibu sana*." (You are welcome.)

"*Chai, tafadhali*." (Tea, please.) Once the *chai* was delivered I said, "*Asante sana*!" And he responded, "*Karibu sana!*"

After breakfast we said *kwaheri* to our new friend Ishmail, and our Maasai warrior. The chef came out along with all the other camp attendants and they all said, "*Kwaheri*," (Goodbye), then we said, "*Asante sana*!" and gave them their tips.

At nine a.m., with Kileo at the wheel in our trusty Range Rover, we departed for the North Serengeti Nyumba, our next camp. The day turned out to be very long and unbelievable! The Serengeti massage was in full ramp; we hit potholes, drove through swamps and mud holes, living and loving the adventure. We saw our first lion (*simba*), lots of elephants (*tembos*), and baboons galore. Vultures sat ominously on trees looking like ornamental Halloween fixtures silently waiting for the next kill. We saw hundreds of birds, including: crowned cranes, a secretary bird, tawny eagles, long-legged storks, egrets, and herons. A female ostrich trotted by, followed in close pursuit by two male ostriches.

We ate lunch perched above a hippo pond; they looked like obese slugs with ears! To get some action going, Kileo made a bull hippo call. Ears and heads popped up in unison like a cartoon.

Kileo informed us, "The hippo is the most dangerous animal of all! They come out of their watery nests at dusk to graze on the grass; if you happen to be in their way they will bite you in two. They are vegetarians but not nice ones. Their enormous jaws are so powerful that if they snap you, you don't have a whisper of a prayer to survive." The message was loud and clear: do not to go anywhere near the hippo area once the sun is setting, and even though they appear to be harmless floating pigs during the day, stay safely in your car!

The most incredible topper to the day was watching the magnificent wildebeest (*nyumbu*) migration from Kenya across the Mara River, into Tanzania. The Great Migration takes place every year. About 1.5 million wildebeests traverse an enormous circle, some five hundred miles, through the Serengeti, seeking new water sources and fresh grasses to graze on. The females birth only one calf, and they, miraculously, all drop within three weeks of each other on one great plain in

Lady ostrich

Hippopotamus

Zebra, leaders of the pack

the southern Serengeti. Just after birth the calves are the most vulnerable to the lions and other predators. Because wildebeests give birth at the same time and in the same geographical area, there are simply too many calves to attack at once. This insures that many babies will live past their crucial early months.

In the area we were in, on the border of Kenya near the Mara River, the wildebeests cross somewhere between September and December. You can make an educated guess, but you will never be sure just when they will cross. They arrive thousands at a time building up a huge herd. The force of the oncoming surge of wildebeests piles up tighter and tighter creating massive tension, until one brave leader takes the plunge down the cliff to the banks of the river below. But, even then, they may frustrate all the waiting 'wanna be' National Geographic photographers. The leading wildebeest may decide today is not the day to cross! Kileo relayed many stories about people making the long journey to Africa three or more times to witness this magnificent natural wonder and missing the crossing. Luck, however, was on our side!

Kileo had not spoken to us yet of the migration, not wanting to get our hopes up. But, it was in his agenda today to check out this particular area of the Mara River and see if there was any action. He parked the Range Rover near some other vehicles, filled with people who had binoculars and cameras at the ready. We waited patiently and watched as the wildebeests proceeded to arrive in droves, forcing the exterior ones to the edge of the cliff. I was terrified that they would be pushed off and be chomped up by the hippos and crocodiles waiting below.

We noticed an interesting phenomenon; zebras in small clusters of four or five were amongst the wildebeests. Kileo told us that the zebras often travel with the wildebeests because the zebras' eyes are good and the wildebeests have a great sense of smell, so they work as a team against predators. The zebras, magnificent in their stripes, were vivid in contrast to the swaths of brown wildebeests. As noted before, zebra is *punda millia* in Swahili, meaning a striped donkey.

Kileo estimated that there were approximately 20,000 wildebeests gathering. To witness wildebeests stampeding into this phenomenal force was an experience of a lifetime! It is considered by some to be one of the seven wonders of the natural world. The tension, the testing, the resistance, and the backing off from making the ultimate decision drove us crazy with anticipation. Then to our amazement from the top of the cliff, six zebras led the migration of wildebeests; once they started sliding down the steep paths to the riverbed below, there was no stopping them.

The first few wildebeests that had slid down the cliff face stopped in their tracks on the shoreline refusing to go into the water. The zebras also tarried on the stone-filled beach, showing no interest in crossing the river. Kileo repeated that sometimes they do not cross, for whatever reason—something spooks them or the current is too swift—so we just waited and held our breath. One brave wildebeest finally jumped into the water followed by another and then another, and soon the Mara river was roiling with a living, moving body of 'beests crossing neck-to-neck and shoulder-to-shoulder.

Another group of wildebeests entered farther upstream and swerved to the direction of the main mass, meeting midway in the water. I couldn't count heads; it was too much of a blur of 'beests. I watched for hippos and crocs; with great relief there were none to be seen. Eventually the original group of zebras casually entered the water; sleek and elegant, they made their own route in a single line across the river, heads held high. They did not enter into the wildebeest frenzy; they carried themselves regally, unlike the spastic, frantic jumps of the wildebeests.

The first wildebeest reached the shore, not far from where we were parked! I had the sudden fear that this incredible force of nature would trample us. Aware that our Range Rover had windows and a roof eased some of my nervousness as I noted that many of the other jeeps were wide open to the elements!

But I had nothing to fear; the wildebeests arrived on shore and stayed on the path in a straight line following the leader. Only one wildebeest stopped and went back towards the water, looking for her calf. Once she found it, they joined in the herd, which was moving at a fast clip past us onto the great wide Serengeti plain. With bated breath we witnessed the entire crossing until the last bedraggled, sopping-wet, wildebeest landed on shore. Kileo revved up the engine and we followed the tail of the herd until they turned to the left, leaving us on the road alone. I wondered how long they could keep up the pace without suffering from exhaustion. I was tired just watching them, but exhilarated at the same time.

It was definitely time to head home for a sundowner and reflect on this magnificent day.

The Great Migration

Waiting downriver

A safe crossing

Kopje

Leopard, Lion, Cheetah, and More!

Monday, October 15

We slept well our first night in our second camp, despite the barking jackals and whooping hyenas. When I heard barking in the middle of the night, I wondered, in my sleep-filled head, why someone would bring a dog on a safari. The next morning I found out that jackals sound just like dogs barking with a high yip. The hyena's *whoooooooooooop* was very identifiable to us by then. Both being scavengers, I think that they were hoping for some leftovers from the camp dinner!

Agama lizard

Another WOW day! It was cool and cloudy as all the mornings had been so far on the northern and eastern Serengeti. Once again, we were glad for our extra gear and warm jackets. But, as the sun rose higher, so did the temperature. Later in the day I wished I had the kind of pants that transformed into cool shorts with two quick zips. We breakfasted and met Kileo by our Range Rover. We were excited for the upcoming day but we were certain nothing could top yesterday's majestic wildebeest migration. We drove to an area in the Serengeti that reminded me of the movie, *The Lion King*. The

Leopard

Greater kestrel

land was flat with tall grass, interrupted by islands of rock formations with sleepy trees growing out of them. This was the perfect place for lions and leopards to hang out unnoticed while rainbow-colored lizards and furry rock hyrax, the size of large rabbits, lazily sunned themselves on the warm rocks. I was entranced by the rock formations called *kopje* (pronounced copy). Their dramatic silhouettes against the plains were like tall ships emerging out of a sea of rolling grass.

Kileo spotted some jeeps pulled over in the shade of a kopje. The passengers were glued to their cameras and binoculars. We edged in tighter, hoping for a peek at whatever it was they were intent on seeing. Sure enough, we saw the leg of an antelope hanging down from a tree, and there, camouflaged by the shadows, a leopard feasting. We had learned from Kileo that leopards are not often found out in the open; once their prey is caught they carry it up in a tree to dine in seclusion. Due to the shadows of the tree it was a bit difficult to see him in his entirety, but just knowing he was up there was a thrill. Kileo, not to be denied, put the Range Rover in gear and backed away to circle around to the other side of the kopje. I guess he had a hunch about where the leopard might appear next. I was afraid we would lose sight of the precious leopard. But Kileo was correct; the leopard, a shy creature, circled to the

Crossing the Mara River

are due. Kileo circled around once more then said, "There are more, we will let her sleep."

The Serengeti massage was in full swing, aching muscles screaming as we drove through more than one steep mud hole after another. As we approached each one, Kileo would holler, "Hold on, just *hold* on." Hold on we did, as we proceeded to drive-slide through the deep mud, the Range Rover groaning and heaving us mercilessly from side to side. The chocolate-colored water sometimes made the halfway mark up the sides of the vehicle. I shuddered to think about getting stuck in the middle. It would be a nightmare. First of all, who knew what was in the water, and secondly, we were not in a populated place with a handy-dandy tow truck. One group we met at camp told us about their axle breaking in one of the mud holes; luckily they climbed out and joined another vehicle. Unlike them, we had no second vehicle. If we got stuck Kileo said he would use his radio to call back to camp, which was maybe a two-hour drive away! But Kileo was an expert driver and our trusty, dusty, Range Rover made it down, through, and back out of every hole we came to.

Another daring feat was our drive across the Mara River, which separates Tanzania and Kenya. Kileo drove to the exactly one-car-width bridge to cross the river. The Mara was narrow at this point and the bridge was simply a flat cement drive over the water. If we stayed too long on the Kenya side we would have no way to drive back across, as Kileo was kind enough to point out, because as the water rises it washes over the bridge and

back of the kopje and sat nestled in the shade of the tree, this time in full view for us to see how gorgeous he really was.

How *did* he get those spots? Our thrill was short-lived however; a greedy vehicle pulled up too close to the leopard, disturbing his peace, and he vanished into the kopje.

As we continued on, leaving the kopje and the leopard behind us...LION! A female lion was taking a nap peacefully on the open plain. We drove up and circled her, rudely rousing her from her nap. She looked at us with little interest; her major motivation seemed to be going back to sleep. She closed her eyes against the ever-constant flies. My stomach gets a little queasy when we are so close to these wild, magnificent animals. I prefer to give them a wide berth and the respect they

Hartebeest, antelope

Oribi, antelope

covers it completely. I wasn't sure we needed this particular kind of adventure but over we went, noting that the water was already tickling the sides of the one lane bridge.

Once across the river we found a grassy, wet savannah bursting with animals, including hundreds of grazing elephants. The matriarch glared at us, raising her long snout high in the air, giving us warning, which I pointed out to Kileo. He laughed and said, "No worry, Donna, I know my elephants and these are not going to charge. Just don't get between a mama and her baby." It was a thrill to see so many of these huge mammoths wandering freely. And there were so many different types and sizes of antelope I couldn't count them all. To my absolute delight, another safari group ahead of us kindly gave us the heads-up that next to the road lay an exquisite African hare in the grass; we would have driven right by, its camouflage was impeccable. There were also giraffes, with the younger ones frolicking as much as giraffes with their long, stretched necks can!

Two feathered female ostriches were busy herding their babies, accompanied by a single male with handsome black markings. Kileo told us that the ostriches have a communal chick-rearing system, where one female and one male raise the whole brood together. How the flock decides who will raise the chicks is a mystery, but this little scenario proved the tradition, since an ostrich only lays one egg at a time and we counted seventeen chicks!

and park toilet facilities were too far away. Luckily, no game wardens or hippos caught our infraction!

Appetites assuaged, we headed back to the bridge. I was anxious to make the crossing, my hands were sweating, and I worried that we had taken too long. Maybe we should have crossed before our lunch. When we got to the bridge we saw that the water had risen and was starting to darken the top of the narrow cement crossing. (If you recall, this was the same river that entertained us with all those floating hippos!) I heaved a sigh of relief as the Range Rover's wheels touched dry land.

Then came the second wildebeest migration! Kileo wasted no time getting us in place for our second viewing of the Great Migration. It was smaller this time and therefore much less dramatic, but we were given a new perspective. This time the wildebeests jumped from the shoreline into water that was only ankle deep, and the results were hilarious! The first one jumped, catapulting high into the air as if its hooves were spring loaded, landing with a splash; the next one, and the one after that, did the exact same comical jump as if it were a contest to see who could jump the highest. Every single wildebeest that crossed the river performed the same jump!

Our contagious laughter at the wildebeests felt like a wonderful tonic. Once we caught our breath and regained composure, Kileo decided it was time to look for cheetahs. We had more muddy crossings and finally arrived at a flat area surrounded by hills. It was threatening rain and the hills were looking dramatic, with sweeps of purplish hues painted over their peaks. We were unlucky in our search for cheetahs, and feeling

African hare

We drove farther into the grassy plains near the official border of Kenya and Tanzania. I spotted a dog, dark and furry; his body was halfway submerged in a pool of water, his head resting on dry land as if it were his pillow. As we grew closer he lifted his head and sat upright, his neck stretched longer than I have ever seen on a dog! But of course he was not actually a dog at all; he was a hyena! He jumped to his feet and joined a pack of other hyenas nearby. One of them had spots and was really ugly, but our guy was bigger and quite furry like a long-necked German shepherd.

By this time our tummies were rumbling, which meant lunchtime. We dined picnic style with a boxed lunch near the bank of the Mara River. Our entertainment was watching forty or fifty hippos floating like slugs in the water. We stayed in the car except for a brief (and I mean *very* brief) pit stop. But we had no choice in the matter; it had been a long morning

Long-necked giraffe

the day had already been a long one, we decided to return to camp. This decision was fine by me; we had been in the Range Rover for almost seven hours.

We'd traveled a good distance when another Range Rover approached on the road. It is an unspoken rule to share sightings when cruising the Serengeti. Kileo asked him about cheetahs and the guide nodded, pointed, and in Swahili told Kileo to go back to exactly where we had been. Ugh! More Serengeti massages as we retraced our tracks back through the mud ruts to the flat plains. My muscles were aching and I yearned to stretch my legs, but my attitude improved the second we saw vehicles lined up near a clump of trees. We pulled into place and grabbed our camera and binoculars. There they were in plain sight: a female cheetah and her three cubs! The female looked like she was sleeping; the only thing moving was her tail, which was long and very black at the tip. Sitting upright next to her was one of the cubs. Her tail went *thwat, thwat, thwat*, and then in one great roll she flipped from one side to the other, landing closer to the cub. She looked up, alert and aware of us spectators, but continued to lie near her cub unperturbed. Suddenly a vehicle nearer to her abruptly started their engine. Why on earth, I don't know, because how could anyone leave this glorious sight? This noise startled her enough to sit upright and take notice. Oh! What a magnificent

Cheetah sitting

Cheetah and cubs

animal! Her markings stood out crisp and sharp; it is an image I will never forget, words could not describe her beauty. A strange joy shot through my entire being. I was in love! Her cub was a miniature, albeit fuzzier, imprint of herself. Kileo's words rang in my ears, "The cheetah is the fastest land animal on earth, a true Olympian!"

I couldn't take my eyes off her sleek yet muscular body! With a riveting gaze and her regal head held high, she rose to her full height and with combined grace and power paraded by with her closest cub. She was soon joined by her two other cubs who had been frolicking, half hidden, in the tall grass. The three strutted in front of their mother, who with intense caution glanced from side to side to check out the distant terrain. By this time I was convinced that the cheetah was the most beautiful creature on this earth. Feeling the sudden onset of rain, the foursome headed in the direction of the far hills. We watched till we could no longer see the black-ringed tips of their tails. With soaring hearts we finally headed back to our welcoming camp.

A true Olympian

LION!

Tuesday, October 16

We woke up to a crystal-clear morning. We had a leisurely breakfast before we piled our gear into the Range Rover and headed out for our third camp, located in the central Serengeti.

It was a long drive through many small villages. There are over two hundred tribes in Tanzania, but the most prevalent is the Maasai. Many boys and men were visible, moving with their herds of cows or goats, their red cloaks worn shawl-like over their shoulders. The children would wave, and some made hand motions at us. We asked Kileo what they wanted; he answered, "They want your lunch!"

Some villages were not friendly about picture taking, so Martin was careful with his camera. Kileo warned him, "This is an unfriendly tribe, no pictures here please. They will grab your camera and smash it. They think you are making money by taking pictures of them. And no pictures of the police station!" He continued, "One guide told his guests not to take pictures and they did anyway. The cameras were all confiscated and the guide was put in jail for a week." We heeded his words, and Martin put the camera in its case.

We turned onto the road that led to our final *nyumba* (campsite). To my alarm, there were crashed trees and broken branches all along the road. Elephant! Kileo drove the Rover with no apparent concern into a cleared section of grass, which was the parking area for the camp. To my consternation I noted numerous small, round bales of hay scattered along the edge of the parking area. These bales were the perfect size of elephant dung! That meant that the elephants roamed awfully close to

Nyumba (Campsite)

Our tent

the tents! To say that elephants are "mammoths" is not an understatement! One hip check or misplaced foot would flatten our tent and us in it. Oh well, I mumbled to myself, nothing to worry about really...the camp has armed guards on duty at night, right?

It was lunchtime and we were ravenous! After so many boxed lunches on the road, eaten inside the Rover,

Mama elephant

Baby elephant

it was a nice change to sit down at a table and be served a yummy, warm, meal of rice with veggies and stewed chicken. We were shown our tent and we were able to unload our gear. The crew, as friendly as always, welcomed us. They were attentive and helpful with the showers whenever we asked. (I was finally getting used to having a man standing outside my tent pouring water into a bag as I bathed, giving him a high sign when I was finished.)

This time we camped with some interesting fellow travelers; some had climbed to the top of Mount Kilimanjaro! They had stories to tell. One told how it snowed during the night and they had to dig themselves out of their tent in the morning. They were proud that they had accomplished this great achievement but also swore they would never do it again! The porters, they said, were wonderful, carrying everything that went with them to the top and back down again. Even with that great help it took all their strength and fortitude to make it. Thompson Safaris boasts of a high success rate of their clients reaching the summit, almost 100% achieve it!

After lunch, we were off in our Rover for another outstanding day! We had a clear view of a leopard lounging, legs dangling down from a tree like a big, limp kitty. More hippos and a huge herd of elephants entertained us. The herd was in the process of lumbering, single file, across the road; all passing jeeps and vehicles stopped to watch the parade. The elephants were taking dust baths. They used their trunks to pick up loose dirt and sand, then raising them high above their heads, dropped the dirt so that it rained down over their backs. One endearing baby elephant following his mother's lead, scooped up some dirt with his nose, as he scampered to keep up with his mama's big steps he proceeded to spray himself with a shower of dirt, covering his ears and backside.

We learned that elephants live for seventy years. They have few predators because they stick together and because of their mammoth size. The only time they are vulnerable is when their babies are small. A lion could take a baby easily, but if there is any sign of danger the elephants surround the little ones, forming an impenetrable circle. The babies scoot underneath their mothers' bellies for additional protection. This hideaway works for the first three years, but after that they are too big to fit under mama. Elephants are also known to help one another; if an elephant gets stuck in a mud hole the others won't quit until the elephant is rescued. As elephants grow old their teeth grind down flat and they can eat less and less; unfortunately, that is the way the majority die, from starvation. It is amazing that these enormous beasts are vegetarians and only eat leaves and grass. I watched in awe as they pulled branches from the acacia tree with fierce needles as sharp as knives and used the very sensitive tips of their trunks to tuck them neatly into their mouths! Kileo told us also that African elephants are not the type you see in circuses. They cannot be trained, or maybe they are too smart to be trained! It is the small-eared Indian elephant that is trainable, poor things.

We were treated to a delightful sighting of two dik-diks. They are the smallest of the antelope, weighing only eight to sixteen pounds fully grown. A fun fact is that these littlest of the antelope mate for life.

And then we saw LION!

A female lioness and two young lions were sleeping under a tree a short distance from the road. Kileo with his eagle eyesight brought us to attention by calling out, "LION!" Our heads spun in the direction that he pointed. Grabbing my binoculars, I scanned the tall waving grasses and spotted a golden paw stretched straight up in the air along with something furry, possibly a couple of ears. Kileo made the call of a baby wildebeest, and one of the young lions, a female, rose up to her full height, stretched in that cat-like way and then headed straight toward us! As she approached our vehicle, I slid down in my seat and closed my window tight. Memories of a YouTube video I'd watched before our trip flashed before my eyes. I replayed the video of a cheetah jumping into a jeep with people in it! I really wished I hadn't watched that video, but it was too late. The image whirled about in my head increasing my anxiety. The lion sat down on the side of the road and yawned a huge yawn, giving us a full show of her fearsome set of teeth and a curling pink muscular tongue, letting us know we had interrupted her snooze. The sun shimmered off her golden fur; she was young, maybe a yearling, and a perfect specimen of health. As Kileo pointed out, she was not hungry; her belly was quite extended from a recent meal. Finding no baby wildebeest or anything else of interest she turned her back on us to return to her pride and her nap!

Lioness

African morning, Serengeti

Up, Up, and Away!

Wednesday, October 17

"*Jambo, jambo,*" our morning wakeup call, woke us from a deep sleep at four-thirty a.m.! Waiting outside our tent was a welcome jug of warm water. The early morning sky was as black as African coffee without cream; the air we inhaled felt crisp and clean. We hurried into our multiple layers of clothing, including hats and gloves, and then found our way to the breakfast tent by flashlight. With an invigorating sip of steaming Kilimanjaro tea and a bite of a Christmas tree cookie for sustenance we began our day. Not exactly our usual chef-prepared camp feast, but we were to enjoy an elaborate breakfast later.

We were instructed to pack our gear into the Land Cruiser; the driver from the balloon company seemed anxious to hit the road. The ride to the balloon launch took a full fifty minutes. I sat next to Jack, an amiable fellow from a small group we'd met the night before. The Land Cruiser was in a different category than our friendly Range Rover; in this vehicle the Serengeti massage felt more like karate chops, rattling our teeth, and making a purée of our tea and Christmas cookie breakfast. It certainly sped up the awakening process!

Once we hit the open savannah we witnessed the most glorious sunrise, its colors ranging from golden oranges to the deepest blue and all the shades in between. The vastness of the African sky without any buildings or artificial light set the stage for a dramatic sunrise/moon setting that couldn't be compared to any other I have ever experienced!

Jack chatted non-stop, sharing his safari experiences. He was in a group of ten people using two Range Rovers. They too, shared the experience of not many pit stops along the Serengeti trail. Jack told of a full day out without a return to camp. It was a hot and dusty day and as a result a lot of water was consumed. Jack and many of the group found it necessary to stop the Rover to kick the tires. He pointed out that with women in the group it had to be done either in two separate spots or at two separate times. They decided rather quickly that the front of the Rover would be for women and the back tires for the men. Just as Jack was descending from the truck, his bladder screaming, a Serengeti ranger pulled up. Only two of the group had the pleasure of release before the ranger's unanticipated arrival! Everyone climbed back into the rover feeling like naughty school children. The two drivers were given severe warning about the fees for breaking the Serengeti commandment, "Thou shalt not leave your vehicle within the park." This is considered as much a safety rule as a sanitary one.

Jack informed me he endured the most painful ride of his life back to the entry of the park where the restrooms were located. A very good rule here would be: when on safari, go before you think you need to, go whenever there is a restroom, and skip diuretics such as coffee or tea whenever possible.

Jack finished up telling his last Serengeti story as we pulled into the balloon staging area. The tip of the rising sun was beginning to send out its early morning rays. We lined up at attention while the organizers called out the rules and procedures for the balloon ride. I noticed that there were rifle-bearing soldiers on guard. A flashback to yesterday! With grave seriousness, we were expected to sign papers agreeing that the hot air balloon company would not be held libel for anything that may befall us on this adventure. That still didn't answer why there were armed guards. I couldn't dwell on it too much because the guide was rattling off how to hook up our balloon security straps, first to ourselves and then to the basket of the balloon. The baskets were lying on their sides attached to an enormous balloon, which was being filled by large and very noisy fans.

My stomach was starting to rebel. I felt like I had drunk turpentine for breakfast and I really didn't care for the taste of it coming back up. I concentrated on my security rigging, strapping myself into it as best I could. Martin and I climbed into the top portion of the basket and lay down flat on our backs hooking our rigging onto the clip inside the basket. It was awkward and ungainly to perform this contortion but we managed and waited while the others followed suit. Once all the sections of the basket were filled the pilot signaled and the basket was pulled upright. Each compartment held four people with four compartments in all, yielding a passenger count of sixteen. The pilot, in the middle, controlled the magic lever creating a flame of fire that caused hot air to rise into the balloon. *Whoosh*, our balloon began its

Sister balloon

ascent into the huge Serengeti sky. *Whoosh, whoosh,* the noise was loud in our ears! The hot flame shot upwards into the balloon lifting us higher and higher.

The view of the sun rising like a great, orange peach was spectacular. The clear crisp air enlivened us and made us eager for this new, once-in-a-lifetime, Serengeti day. The first things we spotted were zebras; they were unaware of us as we floated silently over them. Then with a sudden leap, a gazelle catapulted over the brush with amazing grace and agility, leaving us in awe of its beauty.

We saw our sister balloon climbing higher and higher, as if racing to beat us, but since we were not in a race (nor did we want to be) we enjoyed our gentle pilot and the gliding softness of our ride. It was a thrill to see our own shadow following us as we floated over miles and miles of open land. We descended closer to the ground and came upon water, lots of it, with hippos bathing, soaking themselves, almost completely immersed like enormous floats. Only the tips of their ears, snouts, and round backs peeked above the still waters. Then *whoosh, whoosh* went the hot air and we rose back up again. A huge hippo, unusual to be on his own, splashed knee high through the slender river that led into the lake. We thought he must be a bull hippo, possibly hoping to join in the hippo bubble bath, but first, he would have to challenge the resident bull.

Before we could watch the impending drama unfold we heard the approaching sound of an airplane engine. I glanced down from our floating basket to see the nose, propellers, and wings of a small airplane beneath us. Our mouths fell open in disbelieving gasps as the airplane, having a bit of fun with us, waved his wings and disappeared into the now brilliant blue Serengeti sky.

After that sudden jolt, we were working on regaining a steady breathing pattern, when we heard the word, "Lion!" We stretched to see over the heads of our fellow passengers, who had been on the bottom of the basket during loading but were now in the front row with the best view. One furry brown spec turned into two and three. With focused binoculars and a steady hand, the specs turned into a lion family. A mother and her two cubs were lying in the brush, unaware of our balloon soaring over their heads. Our pilot hovered above the family for a nice long viewing before we glided onwards to our landing destination. By this time the other balloon was down and we could see our path to come. We were the lucky ones, because our pilot was not in a hurry to land; we gently floated for a good twenty minutes longer than our sister balloon.

We touched the ground, bounced once, and then gently skidded for about ten feet to a successful and peaceful landing. We applauded our pilot! Then came the challenge of unhooking ourselves. By now our harnesses were twisted and tangled every which way. Poor Martin unhooked himself and was able to stand upright to his full six feet two inches for the first time since he climbed into the basket; it turns out, his hook and harness gave him less strapping than he needed to be able to comfortably stand to his full height. At five feet two inches I had plenty of strapping, but had turned full circle in the basket so that I found myself in a self-imposed knot.

The basket stands about four feet tall. There are no steps inside or out so it is a hike to straddle the top edge and then a good leap straight down. Martin's long legs easily removed him from the basket, which meant that I could gracefully swing my legs over the rim and slide into his waiting arms. Couldn't ask for a better landing!

We were euphoric! Our bodies were on the ground, but our hearts were still in the clouds drifting over wild

A champagne breakfast

animals and contemplating the magnificence of one of the true wonders of the world, the Serengeti!

We laughed when we were greeted by one of the guides with a huge bottle of champagne balanced on top of his head! Many corks were popped and bubbles were poured into champagne flutes. Orange or passion fruit juice was mixed into the champagne to help settle the bubbles and keep them from going directly to our brains. Feeling light-headed from the adventure, I opted for a heavy hand on the fruit juice. Many did not want the effect lessened and the champagne flowed freely.

Then on to breakfast! The table settings were glorious, covered in dark green tablecloths with white china plates, cups and saucers, real silverware, and matching linen napkins. The sumptuous tables were strategically set under a tall acacia tree that served as a very large sun umbrella. We all chuckled at the humor of having signs on the tables specifying that they were strictly reserved for the balloon travelers. We didn't think there would be too many walk-bys. The servers, handsomely dressed in long white robes and turbans, with dark skin shining in contrast and broad smiles, called out to us, "Welcome! *Karibu, karibu sana*." We were directed to side tables bearing two huge bowls of water and brass monkeys holding bars of soap for us to wash the dust off of our hands. A very classy washy, washy! Nothing was omitted, including crisp, white towels for us to dry our hands.

Once we were all seated the feast commenced. First came huge trays laden with fresh-baked rolls, assorted pastries and fresh-creamed butter, all laid upon our waiting plates by our turbaned servers with great pairs of tongs. Then platters of fresh fruit; pineapples, watermelon, strawberries, passion fruit, mangos, and some I didn't know the names of; were sliced and arranged so elegantly it made my mouth water. And to quench our thirst, besides the fountains of champagne, we were served cold fresh water, hand-squeezed orange

A reserved table

juice, and as much coffee and tea as we could drink.

Fresh eggs were scrambled in huge brass skillets over an open grill along with copious amounts of bacon and sausages. All this savory goodness was served with a slice of roasted tomato, English style. And last but not least, sweet breads and cakes smelling of ginger, cloves, and vanilla arrived on giant platters. The disappointment of our early morning snack of stale Christmas cookies was now long forgotten. Thirty-two balloon passengers plus our pilots and guides ate our breakfasts in ultimate luxury on the same plains that lions roam and wildebeests run!

As we were taking our last sips of tea and munching on one last pastry, all the servers gathered near the road. They began singing "*Jambo, jambo*" while dancing alongside our tables. One server beat a metal cup with a knife another banged a round pan with a metal tong. A hodgepodge of kitchen utensils beat out a contagious rhythm that made us jump out of our seats, clap our hands, and sway our hips to the homemade, handmade, human-made music!

After this storybook balloon and outdoor dining experience, it was time for me to find a restroom. The facilities were separated a safe distance from the dining area, a

Classy washy, washy

Karibu! (Welcome!)

short distance into the bush. As I cautiously approached I saw a sign hanging from a nearby tree, which read, "Occupied." I waited until a person came out and flipped the sign to "Vacant." I flipped the sign and headed toward an esoteric outhouse made of woven sticks. To my chagrin it had only three sides. There was no closure of any kind; the open side gave me a divine view of the Serengeti plains. I couldn't help thinking that a lion might be crouching in the grass ready and waiting for a nice person to eat. (Not a situation where I would want to be caught with my pants down!) The position of the outhouse walls were such that no one could see me from the dining area, and I could see no one, which makes sense from a privacy and a modesty point of view. But I would have traded privacy for some knowledge that others were near. Where was my Maasai warrior with bow and arrow when I needed him? By now I was hopping frantically from one foot to the other, there was nothing to do but to pee, and quickly. I think I could have won a prize for the swiftest gal on safari!

I borrowed the monkey's bar of soap and washed up enjoying the warmth of the African sun. As I returned to join the group I spotted Kileo, who was waiting patiently by the Range Rover, and, as always, smiling! He was ready to take us on another adventure. Out of habit I checked my wristwatch thinking it must be somewhere in the middle of the afternoon. It was ten o'clock in the morning!

Our breakfast umbrella

We jumped into the Rover and exploded with stories, relaying our exciting morning to Kileo. He listened, nodding his head and enjoying our enthusiasm, but let us know that he himself was not big on balloons or any other kind of apparatus that removes one from the solid footing of the earth.

We drove across the waving grass of the Serengeti plains surrounding us, long and expansive and extending farther than the eye could see. The wind, gently blowing, reminded me of what Kansas must look like in the summertime. We were relaxed and taking in the vistas when Kileo spotted them! There were three lions, sleeping in the mid-morning sunshine, their golden brown manes meshed with the long grasses camouflaging them from the naked eye. We would have missed them entirely, but not with Kileo at the helm! He eased the

Silver-backed jackal

Rover to a silent stop and pointed. Unbelievable! We were close enough to not need the use of our binoculars. The threesome lay unconscious and oblivious to us. One lay on his back with his legs in the air. The central one was most visible; with his magnificent markings and full mane dancing in the breeze, making me dizzy with pleasure. These fearsome creatures looked like loveable kittens taking a nap! How could we have flown in a balloon over miles of the Serengeti, eaten a sumptuous breakfast and then be given this gift?

Kileo explained they were young males, who sometimes band together after they are kicked out of their familial pride once they have become too much of a threat to the resident head lion. When this happens they are forced to leave and find a pride of their own. The central lion in the group seemed to be in a drugged sleep when suddenly he opened his eyes and looked right at us. I inhaled deeply in awe of the king of beasts. He kept his eyes open just long enough for Martin to snap a shot of him. It's one of the best pictures he has ever taken!

But our adventures for the day were not yet over... still basking in our luck of seeing the three gorgeous male lions, Kileo gently revved up the Rover and we happily headed back to camp. I was the eagle-eyed spotter this time; there, making his way through the tall green grass was a silver-backed jackal! Quite a handsome specimen, indeed, and he gave Martin a full view and another fabulous photo opportunity.

A young lion king

Jackal

Coffee, African Coffee!

Thursday, October 18

We woke up on our last day at camp to beautiful blue skies. I was eager to begin our day's adventures after finishing a delicious breakfast of pancakes and fruit, washed down by passion fruit juice and tea. We said a few quick *kwaheris* (goodbyes) to the Kilimanjaro mountain climbers we had met the night before, a darling young couple from Davis Square in Somerville, Massachusetts, who said that they had the best trek up and down the mountain thanks to Thomson Safaris. However, they were glad that the strenuous part of the trip was past them and now they could enjoy the delights of the Serengeti. We enjoyed sharing some of our safari adventures with them.

Our final safari destination was beautiful Gibbs Farm, a rolling, flower-filled coffee plantation near the Ngorongoro Crater. I was particularly thrilled because we would be staying in a cottage of our own, in real beds, with running water and electricity! The group we met on the balloon ride had already been to Gibbs. Their itinerary was the reverse of ours. They raved about Gibbs and told us we would absolutely love it. They had lunch there and wished they could have stayed overnight. We were scheduled to have three overnights. I was deliriously happy with the thought!

The ride was long, but there was much to see. We were rattling down the road in our Rover, mesmerized by the prairie grass, when Kileo shouted, "LION!" To me it just looked like grass and more grass, but our super spotter, Kileo, was on target. With the help of binoculars, I saw a paw in the air. Kileo worked his magic and called out in a wildebeest imitation. At least eight heads popped up in a row. The paw that was up in the air never moved, but we could see little ears of cubs and larger heads of medium and full-grown lions and lionesses. It was like a cartoon with sleepy-eyed heads popping up. But a pride of lions woken from their naptime was no cartoon! Kileo called out once more, which prompted a lioness to start moving toward us. Her eyes intent on us as she carved her way through the long grass, she climbed up on a ridge near our Rover and gave us a hard look. I was amazed at the size of her paws; they had to be as large as our breakfast plates! Then, as if we bored her, she opened her jaws

Masked weaver

A lion pride

Ngorongoro Crater

water pressure. I was thankful we were not driving during the rainy season!

As we climbed higher and higher the trees thinned. We snaked along the rim of the Ngorongoro Crater and finally had our first sight into it. Awesome is an inadequate description! The crater had once been a volcano many thousands of years ago. As we drove along the rim, we witnessed the majestic beauty of a natural wonder unfold. Alkaline vapors rose from the crater's floor creating the effect of snow. It was a breathtaking phenomenon: white smoke rising from the crater floor, the sloping hills, the jacaranda trees; the bareness of the outer rim in contrast to the fertile land on the crater's floor made it feel as if it were a delta mirage in the Sahara.

wide in a huge yawn. We sat watching her and she us. We congratulated Kileo; if it weren't for his call we would have driven right by and never known a hidden pride was sleeping alongside the road.

After that excitement we climbed up and up and up, for what seemed like forever. Our Range Rover turned and twisted along roads lined with festoons of light-purple flowering jacaranda trees. Twittering and singing to welcome us were cinnamon-chested bee-eaters and golden-weaver songbirds.

There were paths dug out every so many feet along the steepest parts of the roadside. Kileo explained that they were for the rain. When the rains come, the road would wash away if there was no place for the water to go, so these dug outs were the release valves for the

After an exciting drive along the rim, Kileo informed us that the next day we would drive below to explore the crater. So, for now, it was time to head into civilization and the town of Karatu. As we drove closer to the town, storefronts displayed yards and yards of brightly colored Maasai fabric and bulged with goods for sale. The empty road grew into a major thoroughfare filled with people walking, talking, and carrying baskets of goods on their heads. It must have been market day.

The color of the dirt was a deep terracotta. It looked as though, on rainy days, you could scoop up a clump, throw it on a potter's wheel and, *presto*, you would have yourself a pot. Our eyes darted every which

Fancy boutiques, Karatu

way, trying to capture all the sights. Martin and I both laughed out loud as we passed a particularly colorful cart holding all kinds of sundries for sale. A decorative sign hung on the front of the cart proclaiming its name: Hillary Clinton Shop. We kept driving and soon came upon the Barack Obama Boutique! As humorous as it was; it was heartwarming. I'd felt, throughout the trip, that Americans were welcomed and this reconfirmed my feelings! Everyone we spoke with wanted to know about the upcoming election and their vote was one hundred percent for Obama. In the past, the USA has been kind to Tanzania; John F. Kennedy is much loved for giving money for milk and lunches for the school children when they were starving. It was a nice feeling to know we were thought well of as Americans.

Then onwards to heaven! Gibbs Farm, located just a short ride from Karatu, was our next stop. Kileo drove down a dusty terracotta road passing villagers and their homes made of bush branches glued together with cow dung. We drove past a shop bedecked with enormous black-and-white-striped zebra flowerpots. These pots drew my attention to several men who were busy hand carving wooden monkey chains. I resisted the temptation to ask Kileo to stop. I was too eager to arrive at the gates of Gibbs Farm, which we did a short three minutes later.

We piled out of the Rover, grabbing all our gear. A young man greeted us; he was dressed in a tan shirt and slacks with a red bandana tied around his neck. He announced that his name was Paschalis. Two other men whisked our bags from our grasps. We followed the tall and proud Paschalis down a stone pathway that led us through an enormous garden display of every African floral specimen imaginable. With weaver songbirds twittering above our heads and exotic blooms sending up scents of jasmine and ginger we arrived at our cottage, Mulberry, number four.

The two bellhops wore green tunics and black slacks. I noticed that both of them had two markings on each cheek, like vertical equal signs. It gave them a warrior look. So far in our travels I had not noticed any

A bathroom fit for a queen!

each with its own bookcase and lighted nightstand. My heart thrilled at the charming sitting area with floor-to-ceiling stonewalls establishing a feeling of strength and longevity. The central stonewall sported an intriguing see-through fireplace and cozy leather rocking chairs to sink into on a chilly, rainy day. In the far corner of the room sat a handsome desk and chair placed strategically in front of a large picture window; it offered a spectacular view of the distant rolling hills and the gardens below. I knew the instant I walked into Mulberry Cottage that I was in love. And that was before I'd seen the bathrooms. Yes, plural, bathrooms! After all our rustic restroom adventures, I felt like I had wandered into a French patisserie after being on a strict no-sugar diet.

markings on the Maasai. I assumed it must be a tribal marking, and later on when I inquired, it was confirmed. There are over two hundred and sixty tribes in Tanzania and each one has its own identifications and mother tongue. Tanzania's official chosen language is Swahili; established in an effort to unify the country.

The two men graciously showed us around the cottage and placed our bags on luggage stands. I was in heaven! The cottage was spacious, with French doors that opened to a veranda overlooking the gardens with stunning, blue-flowering jacaranda trees. The porch itself was set up as if it were an outdoor living room with chairs, tables, and all the comforts one would need to enjoy the vista while sipping a cup of tea or a glass of wine.

Once inside the cottage I felt we were in our own private world. There stood two large double beds,

The two-sided fireplace in the sitting room connected with a large bathroom. I peeked through the opening of the fireplace to see what lay beyond. I liked what I saw but soon realized that the easiest way to see the bathroom was to walk through the door. As I entered, I gasped; there sat the most enormous stone tub I had ever seen, carved out of one giant piece of stone. Six people could fit in it! I couldn't imagine how many gallons of water would be needed to fill it. Next to the tub were two handsome sinks with a spacious counter for toiletries. I couldn't resist! I had to run the water. I didn't want to waste it, water being so precious, so after a quick splash I turned it off.

In the corner of the room, there stood a chair with a cushion. It was located exactly where a toilet might be. I peeked under the cushion and found just a wooden

Gibbs Farm

At the farthest end of the bathroom there was a set of French glass doors that opened to a charming outside area. To my surprise, there was yet another shower. The outdoor shower was also open, but it was completely surrounded by a wall of tall bamboo plants. If someone were on the other side, they wouldn't have a clue that anyone was soaping up and bathing in the buff!

We unpacked, freshened up, and arranged for Paschalis to take us on a walking tour of the gardens. We met him at the front gate and he promptly gave us each a walking stick. Paschalis took his job seriously and pointed out each and every vegetable in the kitchen garden. Ninety percent of the food for the dining room is produced on the plantation, including the herbs and spices. In the central area of the garden there was a raised platform built into a tree with spiraling steps leading up to it. This, we were informed by Paschalis, was the elephant outlook. They must constantly be on guard because one visit from the pachyderms would demolish the gardens in microseconds. I wondered if that was why Paschalis gave us such large walking sticks?

After the official tour was complete, Martin and I did a loop around each of the twelve cottages. Flowers bloomed profusely everywhere; each cottage space was bedecked with flowering bushes, creating its own private enclave. The staff quarters were lovely with

seat. I looked around and found another door and opened it. There beyond the door was a room complete with a very private toilet—that flushed—and a ceramic raised sink with a stand and mirror. This bathroom had a window, which was covered on the outside by a wall of garden flowers. I opened the window a crack and bird twitters filled the room. I could spend some serious time in this room! But there was more to explore. I returned to the primary bathroom. A stonewall that held the backside of the open fireplace also sported a showerhead and faucets but with no glass, curtains, or containment of any kind. I looked at the floor. Yes, there was a drain to catch the overflow. This is what I would call an open shower concept!

an ample porch for relaxing and gorgeous sprawling gardens encompassing the buildings. A donkey cart and driver trotted past. We followed along to discover a complete working farm with chickens, pigs, cows, and all the appropriate farm animals. Then, having worked up a thirst and an appetite, we headed in the direction of the main house and grounds.

The main house sat proudly on the top of a rise, with sweeping views over the distant hills. The setting reminded me of Tuscany; the lovely Villa Pitiana, once a monastery, sits on the top of the Tuscan hills like a king's castle. So too, the Gibbs Farm main house sat in regal splendor offering unobstructed views of the rich African landscape. The jacaranda trees in full bloom cast a bluish haze over the farthest hills. Hundreds of birds gave the trees and bushes life of their own. We tarried on the stone pathway that wound around the gardens and the main house. The lawn chairs with plump pillows beckoned us to rest while taking in the view from each progressive angle. We continued onwards, taking mental notes of all the delightful places we might perch once we found our refreshments. We had been told that tea was served anytime during the day. We climbed the steps to the huge wrap-around veranda. There we found plantation guests relaxing in comfortable chairs, drinking beverages, and chatting.

As we took our first steps through the entry, we felt a welcomed coolness of air in contrast to the rising heat of the afternoon. Ah, this old coffee plantation mansion was timeless. I wanted to believe that it had always been here, that no matter what else took place in the outside world, this plantation was here living and breathing! I wanted to touch everything; the tables with old novels, the artwork of the people, the enticing chairs and couches all in supple and natural fabrics, and the wooden floor boards stained a deep coffee brown. The house blended and worked its charm on us as we wandered from one palatial room to the next. In the center of the house we found the heart, a stone fireplace with two leather chairs on either side like thrones. Beyond the fireplace, an open hallway led us to the upper dining room. There, we found not only tea, but also cakes and sweet breads all laid out on the harvest-style dining room table. Just a few steps down from this grand room was a formal dining area with a lovely bay window that gave a delightful view of flowering trees and, beyond that, the working plantation and the blue haze of the surrounding hills.

After our tea, which we sipped on the veranda, we went back to the cottage to change into our dinner clothes. The house and dining room were so gracious we decided it deserved our best attire. It felt good to get out of our safari clothes! We waltzed back to the main house, noting that many more had gathered for cocktails before dinner. Not feeling at all like strangers, we found the bar tucked in the back of the grand room with the fireplace. There we were met with smiles and *jambo, jambo*s. We ordered our drinks and set out to find a nice nook to enjoy them. Outside the grand house we discovered a short flight of stone steps leading us to a completely private seating area. The trees covered us in shade and the weaverbirds sang for us. As we sipped, I realized a blue flower petal had dropped into my wine glass. The petals adorned my hair, landed on Martin's shoulders, and drifted onto my lap. We laughed as we placed our coaster napkins over our drinks! A waiter dressed in a crisp white jacket and slacks, skipped down the steps carrying a full tray of hors d'oeuvres. He greeted us with a hearty, "*Jambo, jambo,*" as he laid the tray on the table.

We answered, "*Asante sana,*" but I quickly added, "we are so sorry we didn't order anything. This must be meant for another party."

Breakfast, first course

his head in an absolute yes and headed back up the steps empty handed. Marty dug into the nuts, and I, more curious than brave, decided to take a nibble of the camel meat. There was nothing that I could discern as meat in the morsel, then the light bulb went on. I got it! I started to giggle calling out, "Camembert! It is camembert cheese!"

Every night servers in white jackets brought a new array of appetizers and every night they were devoured. Delightful! Cocktails and hors d'oeuvres followed by a sit-down homemade meal. Martin was served copper pots full of tangy, fresh-picked vegetables with delectable sauces. I, being the meat eater, enjoyed pots of chicken, pork, and beef, all spiced and grown on the farm. After dinner each night we were lucky enough to catch a glimpse of the very shy but adorable bush baby. The staff fed him bananas as he perched on a tiny platform in the bushes to eat. We were told that they are nocturnal and if we heard thumps on our roof at night, it was most likely the bush babies playing.

That first evening we crawled into our bed relishing the cool fresh sheets, the roof over our heads, the closed door...We drifted off into a peaceful slumber, with no wildebeest grunting, hyena *whooooooping* or jackal barking. Then *THUMP, thump, thump, thump*...my eyes shot open wide and I sat up straight. Martin, sound asleep, made no move to save us. Smiling to myself I snuggled back into my covers, knowing that it was only little bush babies playing!

"No, no, for you." The tray was filled with tempting goodies, but I couldn't tell what their hidden contents might be, so I asked if he could tell us what was on the tray.

He smiled patiently and said what sounded like, "Camel meat."

I tried not to grimace and instead said, "Did you mean camel meat?"

Never breaking his smile, he nodded and said, "Yes!"

I still couldn't quite believe him, thinking to myself why would they serve camel meat in Africa? I thought, Egypt, maybe, but not in this part of Africa. I decided to try pantomime so I drew two humps in the air and saying, "Cammmmel hummmmp?" Smiling, he nodded

The Kill

Friday, October 19

The weather was delicious, sunny, with small, puffy clouds and warm enough to leisurely enjoy our outdoor shower. We dressed in layers, knowing the crater would be warmer than the rim. Breakfast was a smorgasbord of delights: fruit, cereal, meats and cheese, many types of jams, along with bread and muffins all fresh from the kitchen. We were also served juices, tea, and fresh-roasted coffee; we were on a coffee plantation after all! And that was just the first course. For the second course we were offered eggs—fried, scrambled, or poached—hot cereal, pancakes, bacon, sausage, fried potatoes, and on and on…

The smell of coffee permeated the main house; it was roasted every morning. I love the smell of coffee, especially in the morning.

We strolled leisurely past all the blooming flower gardens to find Kileo waiting! "Donna looks happy this morning!"

"Oh, Kileo, Donna *is* so happy! Sumptuous showers, electricity to dry and curl my hair, and being treated like a king and queen, what could possibly be better?"

With a wide smile, Kileo opened the door of the Range Rover. I chattered enthusiastically as I climbed in, "The only thing that could make today better is a trip to the bottom of the Ngorongoro Crater. *Twende, twende, tafadhali*! (Let's go, please!)"

We drove down the red road past the zebra pots. It was quiet this time in the early morning. We passed several Maasai children carrying babies tied in blankets on their backs. They were running and playing as though they had no extra weight. We drove through Karatu and saw the Hilary Clinton and Barack Obama shops all set up, begging passing vehicles to stop and check out their fine wares. After we drove through the main street of Karatu, the ride to the bottom of the crater was a long and twisty one. At every hairpin turn I thought we must soon hit the bottom, but no, not yet! Kileo repeated his favorite expression, "Just hold on! Soon we will be there." I felt like a kid on vacation needing a gas station stop.

We finally reached the gate. Kileo had to fill out paperwork to allow us into the park, which gave us time to stretch our legs and visit the facilities. Then it was back into the Range Rover. Within moments of entering the park we spotted a blue monkey. He really was blue and had an air about himself as if he knew his blueness gained him a high-ranking honor in the world of monkeys. He would have made a perfect addition to Boston's famous theater show Blue Man Group!

Ngorongoro Crater is an oasis supporting a wealth of animal life beyond compare. We soon spotted zebras in groups of two and three standing in close contact with each other along with a huge herd of wildebeests. Big-horned African buffalos stared back at us as we drove by, snapping digital shots of them. Frolicking antelope with twitching tails gathered in swarms all over the crater floor as if it were a giant playground.

Then we saw a laugh-out-loud scene! A male ostrich with coat of black feathers splayed in a huge fan charged, in a gangling sort of way, after a gray-feathered female. At each of several encounters she would dally a bit acting as if he did not exist, then as he came closer she would run away at top speed as if to say, "No sweetie, not in the mood today!" Leaving him standing in the dust with his feathers drooping.

By far the most humorous of all the animals was the warthog. The mother warthog runs along with her tail straight up at a perfect ninety-degree angle from her

A little snack

scratched over every part of his warthog body including under his chin, his sides, neck, back, and legs. The three of us were overcome by contagious giggles when he up and straddled the dirt wall and proceeded to maneuver himself back and forth providing itch relief to all his nether regions. With our windows rolled down we could hear warthog snuffles of pleasure!

We parked alongside the road to watch a herd of elephants using their long delicate snouts to grab hold of the prickly acacia branches and with expert aim stuff the vegetation into their mouths. One gulp and it was gone! How could these multi-ton animals survive on tree salads? It is a mesmerizing sight to behold the magnitude of their beings. And it's such a ponderous thrill to be so near creatures that in a second's time could flip your vehicle upside down!

Kileo dearly wanted us to check off the big five: lion, leopard, buffalo, hippo, and rhino. The first four were easy but the rhino is elusive and endangered. Poachers kill the rhinos for their horns, which are said to have aphrodisiacal powers. Unfortunately, they fetch a high price in the Orient. We were able to say we saw them in the distance on the crater floor, but they were only wavy, gray slivers of a shadow in the distance.

rump. The baby warthogs follow her in the same prancing manner with their little tails in the same position.

The scene we came upon driving down the road in our Rover would have been the absolute winner of the funniest safari video. The scene begins: A warthog lying in a large mud hole enjoying a good soak, another warthog soon arrives to join him. The second warthog wades into the mud up to his belly; he lets go of all his body weight and hits the muddy hole with a splash. Ahh, the healing comforts of a mud bath! We were enjoying the scene when along came another mud-covered hog whose intention was to give himself a thorough scratching against a raised, dried, mud-wall that encircled the mud puddle. He maneuvered himself so that the hardened dirt

Warthog

African buffalo

**** If you suffer from a queasy stomach you may want to skip to the next day! ****

Up until now our animal sightings had been peaceful: creatures snoozing, nibbling plants, frolicking, tails wagging, and even rolling in the mud. But this was about to change.

The most dramatic and the hardest scene of all to witness is the kill. For me it was the most difficult part of our trip; and yet it is the circle of life that goes on day after day all over the world.

In the crater we had witnessed such a plethora of animals that we felt as full and thankful as one does on Christmas morning after unwrapping all the treasures beneath the tree. All of a sudden, Kileo hit the gas pedal and surged forward at great speed. There were twenty or so Jeeps and Rovers lined up along the road in the distant corner of the giant crater. As we approached we could decipher a long dark line of African buffalos, which do not resemble the American bison but look more like a fierce bull. The line was moving forward but there were far too many to count. I assumed this was what the excitement was all about. As Kileo tucked our Rover in between two other vehicles we could sense the tension in the air! Then we saw it: a pride of at least twenty lions, led by several aggressive female lions, stalking the last of the buffalos. My stomach wrenched; the lead lioness looked like she had blood splattered on her neck. The last four of the buffalo turned suddenly and attacked with heads down and lethal horns aimed. Kileo had told us never to be in a buffalo's path; they were mean and they would attack you even though they are vegetarians, like the hippo and elephant. They were sure attacking now!

The lions backed off, and the four buffalo charged again. If the whole herd had charged they would have had an overwhelming chance of scaring off the lions. But, having pushed the lions back momentarily, the buffalos rejoined the end of the moving herd. The drama wasn't over. This time the lead lioness swiftly attacked, injuring one buffalo. I sat down in my seat and groaned. Martin asked if I was okay, and Kileo told me to buck up, this was a spectacular display of strength. I couldn't watch so I turned away, and when I did, I saw a male and a female lion on the other side of the road, lying in the grass enjoying an intimate moment, unaware of the drama unfolding across the road. It was incredible; life was being created at the same time that life was being taken.

The deadly attacks continued between the lions and the four trailing buffalos. The lions proved amazingly cunning and patient. They focused on one buffalo; we decided it was an older one and easier prey than the others. The poor buffalo finally fell and the lions pounced and feasted. The other three buffalos abandoned the scene, running to catch up with the herd once there was no longer any hope of saving their companion.

I felt sick to my stomach. But, I had to admit, it would have been harder to witness if the prey had been a gorgeous zebra or a Thomson gazelle!

As we departed, Kileo told us that by the end of the day there would be nothing left of the buffalo but bones. Hyenas and jackals would follow the lions, and then the vultures would finish up, thus preventing any rotting or festering of the flesh. This was nature's way of keeping the crater floor clean.

After the exhausting emotion of the kill, we found a lovely spot by the hippo pool to rest and revive ourselves with a boxed lunch. Amazed that I was starving, I dug into my picnic lunch with gusto!

As we chomped on our cold chicken, Kileo told us the story of the stupid man who was warned by his guide not to feed the birds, as they can be quite aggressive. After these wise words were spoken to him he placed a piece of chicken on his head! The tawny eagle, a beautiful bird, swooped down, snatched the chicken with his talons along with part of the man's scalp. That was the end of his safari! He was emergency airlifted to the nearest hospital. We wisely ate our boxed lunch inside the jeep!

**** It is okay to resume reading for those with queasy stomachs! ****

Gibbs Farm, Day Two

Saturday, October 20

Our second day on Gibbs Farm was slated to be a non-safari day. We took our time in the morning, sleeping in just a little and enjoying the lovely outdoor shower. I was ridiculously happy to have the time to use my magic wand and curl my straight locks. We wandered into the dining room of the main house to sample all the delectable morning treats. Once again the table was laden with fruits and breads, jams and spreads, teas, and of course the robust freshly roasted coffee. After the goodies, the server with a huge smile came to take our order! Eggs, bacon, sausage, pancakes, omelets, you name it, cooked fresh just for you.

I loved every second of walking the grounds, listening to the birds, and enjoying the countless varieties of flowers bursting with blooms everywhere. The land must be extremely fertile on the outer rim of the crater. I think I could live on Gibbs Farm very happily!

The morning's agenda was to visit Daniel the storyteller. While Daniel was dramatic, he wasn't what I would consider a storyteller, but rather a bearer of history and culture. He knew more about American history than I did. As it turns out Daniel was a retired history teacher and his specialty was teaching American History. He spoke extremely highly of John F. Kennedy. He said that when Tanzania was starving, President Kennedy did much to help stave off the hunger. Through Kennedy's efforts and our tax dollars, the children were provided with lunches in all the schools. For most, that was their only meal of the day. Today Tanzania is still counted as one of the poorest countries in the world.

Daniel led our small group to a replica of an original home of his tribe, the Iraqw. The house was an underground dwelling; from the road you couldn't see it. On the side pointing away from the road there was an entrance made of cut trees. Upon entering the house we found it to be very dark, taking awhile for our eyes to adjust. Daniel's wife, Elizabeth, showed us how they ground flour from wheat kernels by scraping the stone back and forth. It looked like a long and arduous process to get enough flour to make a loaf of bread, let alone feed a family. Daniel pointed out that this was woman's work!

The family slept above the floor on lofts made from cut trees; downstairs housed the cattle and goats in separate pens. So cozy! A long, spear-like rod stood by the door to be used in case the Maasai came to steal the goats. The idea is to camouflage the underground house so the passing Maasai would not know they are even there. The Maasai believed all cattle belonged to them. If they discovered the entrance they would attack to reclaim the animals they believed belong to them, but

Underground dwelling

Daniel's chickens

Daniel's tribe mates would be at the ready. Daniel demonstrated how to thrust the spear and he was quite dramatic, shouting loud chants and showing courageous outrage. I wouldn't dare try taking Daniel's cattle!

Back at Gibbs we relaxed and enjoyed a lovely lunch outside on the terrace. Our view was enchanting and the birds twittered to us from the burgeoning flowerbeds. It was a little piece of heaven on African soil. Suddenly, Martin, relaxed to a point of no return, tipped backwards in his chair. Once in motion there was literally no way to stop gravity. I gasped in horror as I watched him fall! In a split second he was flat on his back with his feet in the air—not an easy position to get out of, with the arms of the chair trapping him sideways. The top of his head missed the surrounding stonewall by a hair's width. He would have been knocked unconscious if his head had hit. We eventually got him detangled and he recovered with a flushed look on his face. Our luncheon neighbors jumped up to help, but he assured all of us that he was perfectly fine as he brushed leaves and flower blossoms from his shirt. The garden was left with a sizeable dent in it. I later gasped when I saw the huge purple bruise on his back. There we were sleeping with hyenas and cavorting with lions and the garden chair almost did him in!

That afternoon Paschalis took us on a walking tour of the village. He greeted us, once again with walking sticks and a bottle of cold water. The sun was high and hot. We wore our kerchiefs and I was glad of it.

A house in the village

Empty schoolroom

The burnt sienna dust on the road was thick, offering a contrasting glow to the deep green of the trees. We found the red dust was everywhere: on our shoes, on the bottoms of our slacks and socks, and when the wind blew, red clouds of swirling dirt stuck to our sweat giving us a terra-cotta glow.

We passed children playing while minding small goats. As before, some of the children had slings holding babies on their backs. Two happy-faced girls raced in tandem with babies' heads bouncing up and down with their strides. I worked hard to keep pace with long-legged Paschalis as he talked about village life and how elephants can take down a village in one pass. He told us they don't usually trample the houses but they do decimate the gardens. The villagers use prickly acacia tree branches to make barriers, but Paschalis said that the elephants plod along wherever they like and it is nearly impossible to stop them—and it is against the law to shoot them.

We reached the school, but it was Saturday and it was closed. Two schools now and both closed. I must admit I was disappointed because I longed to see the school children. We walked through the empty rooms, spread out in long buildings that reminded me of army barracks. The classrooms were cleaner and neater than the Maasai school we saw in the Serengeti, but the meager, wooden benches with slant-top tables looked stiff and unwelcoming. Paschalis explained that many people from America and Canada who come here as tourists donate money to the school. There were many plaques stating that such and such a corporation or group gave this playing field or painted and repaired that classroom. Thomson Safaris gave the villagers free water by building them a well. Paschalis said that tourists are good for Africa and they need them for the dollars they leave behind.

We left the school and headed back to the road that led to Gibbs Farm. Paschalis stopped at a house that made liquor, but the owners were not home. Paschalis told us that home brewing was very popular and

A full schedule

inexpensive, which made it easy to obtain. I didn't get the feeling that Paschalis partook in this pastime, nor that he approved, but I guess he thought it worthwhile to add to our tour.

As we walked back down the red dirt road, we were passed by a long line of women dressed in colorful shawls and scarves that covered their heads and shoulders. We couldn't help but notice the beautiful fabrics that adorned them. One group of women stopped and greeted Paschalis. They spoke to him in Swahili and asked, "What are your guests saying about us?"

Paschalis, interpreted and then he answered for us, "My guests say that they understand that when you wear your head scarf it is an important occasion." They seemed pleased with the answer. I asked if the special occasion was a wedding. Paschalis told us, no, it was a funeral, and it had been going on for days. A young woman in the village gave birth to a child and then she bled to death. He said that this is a common cause of death for young women. I had to wonder if the reason for so many deaths by childbirth is because the women are really girls and too young to be having children? Or, is it lack of proper medical care? Or both?

We walked past a line of village folk in front of a huge black tank, the one that Thomson supplied. They were waiting patiently for their turn to fill their jugs. Paschalis told us there is no running water in the village and that all water must be carried in. Firewood also needs to be gathered every day for cooking. He had a contemplative look on his face as he stated, "This is our life!"

By the time we made it back to Gibbs, the temperature must have been well into the high nineties; I was ready for a cold shower to wash off both the sweat and the red dust. I felt a wee bit guilty taking that shower when the village people have no plumbing at all, but I remembered being told upon arrival that all our water from our use was saved and reused to water the plants in the vegetable garden!

A home distillery

Dust Devils

Sunday, October 21

This was our last few hours on Gibbs Farm. As we walked to the dining room the weather promised to be hot and dry with some forceful winds.

Sadly, after a delightful breakfast of eggs and bacon, toast and jam, fruit and juice with tea, and the smell of coffee roasting, we said *kwaheri* to Gibbs Farm. We had a nice chat with Tracy and Peter, the managers, before we loaded the Range Rover. Kileo was to drive us to the airport in Manyara, but first we made a stop at a tourist store along the road to see the famous tanzanite. It was very beautiful, a delicate range of colors from white to purple. These beautiful gemstones are found only in Tanzania. However, 1,600 American dollars for a piece of unset jewelry was out of the budget.

We arrived at the airport. Kileo located the woman in charge and we were checked in. It was hard to say *kwaheri* (goodbye) to Kileo; we had spent eleven days on the road with him, as our companion, tour guide, protector, and *rafiki* (friend)!

Since there was nothing to do but wait, we walked around outside the tiny waiting room. There were a few stalls with typical African bric-a-brac. As I entered, a young man approached me, greeting me in English. He proceeded to show me things on the shelf and tried to place them in my hands. I did not feel at all comfortable so I shook my head no, I told him I would just like to look. He only became more adamant, and insisted that I should like this object, and if not that, then this one. I asked him to please stop bothering me! But he only became more aggressive, absolutely insisting I buy something because he needed the money. I said NO and to stop it! I would not buy anything from him. I walked out of the stall, with him trailing behind me openly begging with tears in his eyes. Martin came over, now aware that the man was harassing me, and sent him away, the young man left but with angry words.

I walked across the dirt road to a tiny booth with some small food items. I spied a box of Kilimanjaro tea, which I had enjoyed every morning in Africa. I picked up the box, but did not find a price. (You'd think I'd have learned from my immediate past experience, but no, I asked for the price.) The young man said fifteen dollars. I replied, "No that cannot be correct! That is too much money for a box of tea bags!"

He answered, just one minute, and came back with a slightly older man. The man said he was very sorry, the boy was wrong—the tea was only ten dollars. I laughed and said, "Never mind, I will find tea somewhere else." I turned to go back to wait for the plane in the tiny airless room. He followed after me, and said ten dollars is good price, but I could have it for eight dollars and that was giving it away. I said no, I was not interested, and now I was really becoming quite annoyed. He persisted, so I said I would give him three dollars; that was it, tops! He countered with five dollars. Now, worn down, and still wanting the tea, I said okay. I handed him a five-dollar bill, thinking to myself, it had better be good tea. I brushed the red dust off the shiny cellophane paper covering the box. Later in the trip, in another airport gift shop I saw the exact same box of tea for three dollars. Oh well, the tea was excellent and it was so strong we could make a whole pot from just one bag!

Our plane ride to Arusha was a hair-raising flight! It was a small plane, filled to the brim with safari folk. The pilot, being a bit of a dramatist, announced that we would start our trip by flying off a cliff. He was not kidding. The airstrip was on top of a tall plateau and when it ended we were in the air! I yelped with surprise at the stunning view. The plane swooped low, hovering over magnificent Lake Manyara. Thousands of flamingoes flew in long pink formations across the enormous lake. We cried out with sheer pleasure at the magnitude and wonder of it all!

We had hardly finished passing over the lake when we hit the dust devils! They were mini red tornadoes, five hundred or so feet up in the air! Twirling and churning, these devils swept down and across the red-hot African soil. It was terrifying! We stared frozen out our small plane window as one after another of these dust devils grew more and more threatening. The ride that started out to be a feast for our eyes was now a challenge for our poor stomachs. The plane bumped and lurched for the full twenty nightmarish minutes to Arusha. When we landed the pilot said he was sorry it was such a rough flight. I shuddered at the thought of getting back on another plane, which we had to do to fly to our next destination, the beautiful spice island of Zanzibar. Maybe we should call it a day, be content with our costly purchase of the five-dollar box of tea, skip the Spice Island, and head for home!

But luck was with us; the next plane was a good deal larger and newer-looking. The captain was a woman! Those of us who had transferred from another plane looked a little gray in the gills. The pilot immediately relieved our worries, "There are dust devils around Arusha caused by the heat and the high gusts of wind. We will be flying over some, but we will be at a much higher altitude and once we are over the water the dust devils will disappear and the flight will be smooth." With a *whoosh*, we were up and over those nasty dusty devils in no time, and soon we were looking down upon the tranquil turquoise waters of the Indian Ocean.

After a little over an hour we started to descend. We could see that the population was growing denser and denser. From our perspective, the view below looked like tiny tin matchboxes placed in rows. I wondered if it was some kind of technical plant or perhaps an indoor hydro garden? I soon realized that it was the rooftops of the houses that the people of Zanzibar lived in. The streets were extremely narrow and many of the houses had common walls. There wasn't a pinch of green anywhere. It looked like an oven.

Our plane landed and we grabbed our duffle bags and walked to the lobby of the airport. All the women wore long robes with no part of the body showing except their sandaled feet, fingers, and facial features. A few wore the burqa, a full veil with only a slit for the eyes. Most wore the Muslim scarf, which covered their heads

Dugout canoe, Indian Ocean, Zanzibar

and necks, revealing only their mouth, nose, and eyes. All the clothing was dark, mostly black, and I thought of how hot they must be, especially those who were in their hot-flashing fifties. Even in the air-conditioned airport, dressed in loose white pants and a light cotton blouse, I was glowing!

Our driver found us immediately and ushered us out to the awaiting vehicle. He seemed so happy to see us, like we were long-lost friends. He gave us each a frozen bottle of water, and I mean a frozen solid bottle of water, which we gratefully accepted. Then with great ceremony, he presented us with two frozen washcloths, rock-hard frozen, stiff as a board! We chuckled as we climbed into the back seat of the van. It was only moments before the washcloths started to defrost, dripping all over us! The frozen water bottle took a

Fishing boat, Indian Ocean, Zanzibar

while, but eventually we could suck some liquid from the mini glaciers.

Our guide/driver talked non-stop the entire trip. His favorite phrase was, "Take picture, take picture!" He told us that some things are not okay to take pictures of so he would let us know which ones were okay. We weren't to take pictures of people or their houses or people in the brightly colored markets that we passed. Martin took all the ones he suggested and practiced restraint the rest of the way. It was a long drive, longer than we thought it would be. Our destination was the tip of the island, which was the entire length of the island away.

We eventually drove through the little village of Nungwi and soon arrived at our resort. At first glance it held the promise of pure unadulterated paradise! At the entrance we were flagged to stop by a man in a very official-looking uniform. He asked for identification and the driver provided the necessary proof that we were indeed guests at the Ras Nungwi Resort. We were ushered inside a gorgeous lobby with a succession of high-peaked ceilings made out of timbers lashed together tiki style. We were asked to sit. It always seemed that we were seated with much ceremony while registration took place. We sunk into the lovely pillows of the welcoming couches and were immediately brought two cups, made out of coconuts, boasting tropical blooms and straws for sipping the tempting contents. Ahhh, the life of the rich and famous! I was ready to bathe in it.

After we were properly signed in, a bellhop in tropical attire grabbed our bags. The manager, an English-speaking woman, instructed the bellhop to deliver them while she gave us the royal tour. I tried not to let my jaw drop as we walked the sweeping paths and steps leading us through the internal world of Ras Nungwi Resort. The interior foyer was lined with

Ras Nungwi Resort, Zanzibar

huge couches and heavy, wooden coffee tables; their tabletops were carved in designs reminding me of the African marble game, mancala. The dining area was covered with the same vaulted ceilings and surrounded by a low, woven wall. Other than that, all other spaces were open to the elements. And the elements were gorgeous! Pathways wove in and out between the guest huts with plants and vibrant flowers everywhere giving a lushness of the tropics. Sweet sculptures of bronzed cranes and comical prancing warthogs pleased us along the walk to the pool and to the deck overlooking the Indian Ocean. The sandy, white beach was peppered with hammocks and decadent reclining chaise lounges. Piles of fluffy, rolled towels were waiting to pamper us, while refreshing beverages were available at our beck and call. A bar built to perch out over the ocean offered a particularly stunning view.

We walked on and on past the empty *dhows* (pronounced dows, rhymes with cows) moored in the turquoise water. The entire resort rested on a peninsula

Our stepladder to the beach

around which wrapped the turquoise waters of the Indian Ocean.

Our guide directed us to our front steps. Our abode was completely round, with a porch and door on one side mirrored by a porch and door on the other, splitting the living space into two half residences. Our porch was glorious, fully outfitted with a couch, chair, and table. Here we could sit and meditate on the loveliness of life, with nothing between the Indian Ocean and us. Directly in front of us were two dhows floating on their moorings, like a landscape painting waiting for its master! Inside, the bed was center stage, with tons of pillows and a fluffy bedspread bedecked with fragrant bougainvillea blossoms. Our room also sported a handsome hardwood desk, and on it, a bouquet of flowers with a personalized handwritten welcome note. We found a basket of snacks and a fridge filled with cold drinks. The bathroom was a step up and state of the art; flower blossoms crowned the roll of toilet paper and adorned the bars of soap and sink top!

Tired from our travels we yearned to stretch out on the bed, but we garnered new energy from our surroundings and quickly slipped into our bathing suits. We climbed down the steep wooden rungs of the ladder in front of our abode leading us to a sandy beach and the sea. The beach itself was wide and went on forever. We walked it, not ready for a swim until we climbed back up from the beach and our eyes rested upon the beautiful pool, which telegraphed us an engraved invitation for a refreshing dip. Swimming in a pool while watching fishermen in dhows with enormous white sails billowing across the turquoise sea was most extraordinary, I reveled in the fact that I was somewhere in the world I had never been before, a world called Zanzibar!

After our invigorating swim, we rested on the comfy chase lounges and had almost dozed off to sleep when my tummy started talking to me. The sun was setting and I realized it was near dinnertime.

We went back to our semi-circle dwelling. I showered and changed into a lightweight cotton skirt and blouse for dinner; Martin donned his collared shirt and long pants. By then it was romantically dark as we wound our way through the meandering paths to the enticing evening dining room. Guests were streaming in from every direction, gathering under the twinkling lights of the lounge. A band dressed in multi-colored tunics and turbans were singing and playing large conga drums, guitars, and multiple other instruments. The sound of the music quickened our step, making us groove to its beat. The waiters were ready to take drink orders, and eager to teach us how to play the games on the carved tabletops. When all the guests seemed to be settled in, a gong rang out and another set of waiters in long white robes and white turbans appeared, clapping their hands, swaying to the rhythm, and singing for us to follow them into the dining hall. It was more fun than Ma on the farm ringing a bell! We were swiftly led to our seats and the dining began. The lights and stars sparkled and our romantic evening with a table set for two was simply divine!

Muslim School

Monday, October 22

We woke up with the sun streaming into our ocean front villa. It was dreamy to peek out the windows and see our favorite dhows swaying with the motion of the sea. Paradise!

Breakfast included everything you could possibly desire: savory dishes steamed, roasted, grilled, or custom cooked just for you! Accompanied by a smorgasbord of cereals, rolls, cakes, breads, butter, jams, fruit of every description (to name a few: bananas, mangoes, pineapples) and we could fill our plates as many times as desired. The waiter came and bowed in his long white robe and caftan. Proud of my Swahili, I greeted him and asked for tea please. "*Jambo, jambo, chai, taffadalli.*" He smiled ear to ear and graciously retrieved a pot of tea and two cups.

After a leisurely breakfast, we met Roger, the headwaiter, who would be taking us on a walking tour of the nearby village of Nungwi. We arranged a time and meeting place and went back to change into city clothes. Shorts and swimsuits are fine in the resort, but when outside I was instructed by Thomson to cover up with loose, modest clothing. Martin never had a problem with what to wear; he donned his slacks and polo shirt. Men in Zanzibar dress like anywhere else: jeans and T-shirts, or slacks and shirts. Women are the ones who must be covered up in Muslim culture, so it was my concern to dress appropriately. I picked a skirt that came below my knees and a blouse with sleeves. It was hot and steamy in Zanzibar, much more so than on the mainland. I would learn later, however, that the more clothes the better.

Teacher and classroom of students

A car appeared and Roger motioned for us to climb in. It was a short drive to the village and once there we could go on foot. Roger explained that the primary school was closed due to exams, but thank goodness, the nursery school was open. We carried a bag full of pencils, crayons, chalk, and writing books to give as a thank-you present to the school for our visit. We were first ushered into a playground area. I noticed it didn't have swings or any type of climbing apparatus, but the ground was well worn from many little feet running and playing games. From the outside, the school looked more like a commercial warehouse than a nursery school. We entered through a short hallway; there were slipper-style shoes flung everywhere, not in rows, nor in pairs, but scrambled like the shoe scramble game we played as youths at parties.

The hallway opened up into two large classrooms. The one to the left was loud and at a near riot-level of frenzied activity. Roger told us that one was the older class; we were to visit the younger one, which was calm in comparison. A young teacher in full scarf and long sarong greeted us. Roger spoke in Swahili and then translated back to us. The children sat in rows on the floor with the boys in the front and the girls separated by a space in the back. I counted twenty-nine boys and thirty-six girls. The boys' heads were shaved short and some almost completely bald. They wore school uniforms of dark blue shorts and light blue shirts. The girls were breathtaking in light blue head veils and long blue dresses to the floor. Their head veils came down past their shoulders with their alert brown faces shining through a circular opening so you could see eyes, nose, mouth, chin, forehead, and maybe a trace of hairline. They were all barefoot, including the head teacher and the assistant teacher. I wondered if we should follow the rules and take our shoes off, but Roger kept his on so we did, too.

The head teacher was tall and thin with a regal stride and total command of the children. She was in the middle of a lesson and stood in the space between

The students were curious

the boys and the girls. She did not stop her lesson to greet us or introduce us to the children. They, however, were curious about us!

The children chanted in a singsong style after their teacher, first their letters and then their numbers. When they counted they held up their baby finger for the number one and on to the thumb for number five. We were amazed how well the children behaved as the teacher first sang the letter or number and they followed her lead. Then, as I was about to proclaim them all angels, the teacher turned her back on the girls to return to the front of the classroom. In that split second, a hand shot out grabbing the veil of her neighbor and gave it a good yank. The girl righted her headpiece and with a tight little fist and accurate aim, clipped the offender right on her chin. Full of grace, the teacher turned to continue her lesson. The girls were both sitting chanting their numbers with angelic looks on their faces. It was hard not to burst into a fit of giggles; they were just like kids anywhere!

We asked if we could take pictures and the assistant teacher gave her permission with wave of her hand. Martin was able to capture the essence of their curiousness about us: their beautiful dark eyes searching, wondering who we were, and why we had entered their world. I was so excited to finally be in a classroom with children in it and to experience a tiny part of their life. Roger told us that these were the lucky ones. The parents must pay for education and having the privilege to attend nursery school gives them a head start for the demands of primary school. The unlucky ones stay home and take care of their younger siblings.

Open market

At the end of a delightful visit we gave our bag of goodies to the assistant teacher; she happily checked out our offerings. I had already realized that these children did not use pencils or paper but hoped they would share with the older classroom. We said, "*Asante sana, kwaheri*," and then walked out into the bright sunny world of village life.

The village was alive! We stopped in a small grocery store; it was neat and tidy and made me want to buy something. I settled on a box of ginger tea and paid a very reasonable price with Zanzibar currency. We strolled down a well-trodden dirt road that I guessed must be the main road. Women were busily weaving huge palm leaves into mats. Stacks of palm fronds were laid out to dry on the shady part of the road. They smiled at us as we passed. The mats looked like they might be woven into something bigger. Sure enough, just down the road, there was a yard totally enclosed by the same woven mats.

As we strolled, we passed many small workshops with wide-open doors. We watched as carpenters assembled their newest piece of furniture. Children played in front of the shops, older ones minding the younger ones. Upside-down pineapples hung in many tiny bays along with other fruit and food items that I didn't recognize. Sewing machines buzzed, making sack purses from brightly colored fabrics. Women covered from head to toe, allowing only their faces to be seen, carried big, colorful plastic tubs on their heads to the water site. One woman who passed us stopped when Martin aimed his camera toward a group of women, she strongly insisted in Swahili that we were not to take any pictures of them. And yet another woman down the road posed for us to take a picture. Roger explained that some

The village beauty salon

do not mind if we take pictures, but others feel we come to take pictures to make money from the photographs and others simply do not like strangers taking pictures of them. We obeyed and thoroughly enjoyed our short time in the little but bustling village of Nungwi.

Roger was eager to take us to see the boat-building yard and the fish market, so we turned from the main road and headed toward the beach. The dhows were built one at a time and assembled completely by hand. From where the new boats were perched, we could see the white sand and turquoise water of the Indian Ocean. Children frolicked and played on the sand near the water, I didn't see a single adult around them. Their happy sounds filled the air.

The sand infiltrated my sandals, making me itch to take them off and walk along the waves breaking on the shore. But, instead, I stopped stock-still and caught my breath! There was a man sitting in the sand and on his lap was a miniature dhow with tools spread around him on the sand. Martin was already fast approaching him. The man never looked up as we charged in his direction. The miniature boat was maybe ninety percent finished. It was a true replica of what we had already fallen in love with, the image of a picturesque dhow rollicking in the waves.

Martin asked Roger if he would ask the man if it was for sale. Roger asked in Swahili and the man answered that it wasn't yet finished. Roger translated and Martin said we could come back later, maybe tomorrow. Roger translated and the man seemed disinterested and shook his head no. Martin really wanted to buy the boat so he persisted and said he would pay him for the boat now if he would sell it to him. Roger said, no, that it was not a good idea. I agreed with Roger; the man might not show up with the finished boat and there would be nothing we could do. Martin asked Roger to tell the man that we were staying at the Ras Nungwi Resort and we would really like to buy the boat. Finally the man spoke directly to Roger and said, yes, he could finish it tonight. He would bring it to the resort the next day.

A friendly face

Beach boat builder

He would need to be paid in cash. Roger asked him what the price would be, and the man answered, fifty dollars. We readily agreed and the man finally smiled but still said nothing to us directly. Roger thanked him and we gave him our name on a card to present at the hotel. He could not give us a time that he would come, so we said we would leave the money at the desk with instructions that he should be paid when he delivered the boat. Whew! It took a lot of negotiating but we were giddy with the hope that he really would show up with the finished boat. Roger seemed very skeptical!

With miniature dhows dancing in our heads, we headed toward the fish market. The fishermen had tarps on the sand, filled with piles of thin, silver fish. There were a lot of flies buzzing around making the market not all that appealing. Roger explained that the silver fish are what the villagers commonly ate. They were very good fried on an open fire. Roger told us that the villagers did not eat the fancy fish that we were served in the resort. They were too expensive for the locals to eat!

The fishermen seemed sleepy; there wasn't much action selling fish. Several of the men slept on the

Fish market

tarps next to piles of freshly caught fish. One man was sitting upright and staring in my direction. As we approached I realized he was staring at my legs, his eyes were penetrating, boring holes through my skin. I immediately felt self-conscious and walked away. I could still feel his eyes long after we were out of his range of eyesight! I then wished I had worn a full-length skirt and a long sleeved blouse.

Once away from the fish market Roger steered us in the direction of the aquarium. It was a great way to finish our village tour. We had a young and very enthusiastic guide who gave us a fabulous tour. It was not a huge facility but rather a couple of buildings and a dock to a pond. The most exciting attraction was the sea turtles! There were big ones and small ones that, unafraid, swam right up to the side of the dock to greet us. Our guide called out their names as they surrounded the dock. All the turtles were rescued from fishing nets or were wounded in the sea by other creatures and had washed up on the beach. Our guide explained that some of the sea turtles would recover enough to be placed back into the sea. Others, who would be at risk, would stay on and be taken care of.

We returned to our resort and decided we had to

Rescued sea turtle

take a ride on a dhow! We quickly signed up for the three-thirty to seven o'clock cruise. We showed up in our bathing suits and beach towels eager with anticipation. A young couple from London, Charlotte and Chris, whom we later learned were on their honeymoon, joined us.

Our first adventure was the walk out to the boat! I had assumed we would be rowed out to the dhow, which was moored some distance away, but I was wrong. The tide, luckily, was low; we watched the crew walk out with ease to put supplies in the boat and return to fetch us. Single file we took our first few timid steps into the vast Indian Ocean. The water twinkled in the late afternoon sun. It was solid sand under our feet, not squishy with turtle grass or slimy seaweed. We forged onward, holding the camera and towels above our heads as we hit waist deep water. When we reached the boat a crewmember extended his hand to haul us over the side and into the body of the dhow. Once on board I felt as if I had swum the English Channel, or at least a small walking version of it.

The crew introduced themselves as captain and first mate. The captain had a huge winning smile that insured great confidence in his seamanship. He talked a little about the boat and invited us to either stay

Martin the sailor

down on the main deck, or if we liked, we could climb the ladder to the uppermost level. I was surprised we could climb up there; it looked like a simple platform to cover the deck, and it was higher up than I cared to climb. Martin scrambled up the ladder followed by Chris and Charlotte; I lingered below feeling safer in the more substantial part of the boat. But, as the crewmen were busy getting the boat ready to sail, I felt in their way, so I built up my courage and ascended the ladder. When I got to the top I was ready to high tail it right back down again. But Charlotte seemed relaxed, and Martin encouraged me, so I climbed from the ladder to the platform. And that is exactly what it was, a platform with a miniscule railing, maybe eight to ten inches in height. Not nearly enough to prevent us from plunging over the side! I could feel the boat starting to move with the waves. I inched myself across the floor on my bottom, to sit next to Charlotte. Martin, who is not afraid of heights and had sailed the seven seas as a youth, was in heaven, standing upright and taking pictures from every angle.

The Ras Nungwi resort is on the absolute tip of the island. As we rounded the top-most point, we found ourselves heading into open seas and choppier waters. The sail was full and we flew south along the coast. It was exhilarating: the sights of other dhows passing, filled with fish and fishermen, hotels and resorts looking like mosque temples, and white sandy beaches peppered with bronzed bodies. Our sail, with a great blue dolphin painted on it, billowed and caught the wind, carrying us farther from shore and into the deeper parts of the sea. The boat lurched to a dizzying forty-five degree angle; Charlotte and I scooted over to the higher side of the platform and grabbed hold of the railing. I yelped in terror! Charlotte called to Chris, “This was supposed to be romantic. This isn’t fun!” Feeling the same way I called to Martin to come sit near me. He gallantly came and positioned himself so that if we went over, he would be first. Unless, of course, the boat tilted to the other side!

We all caught our breath, giggling nervously as the boat leveled. The crew below seemed unconcerned with our whoops and hollers of panic. They kept the dhow clipping at a good speed. I guess when they have the wind they go with it. We relaxed, gradually, and started to chat when Martin noticed his camera was sliding sideways heading for the other side of the dhow. He pounced on it, saving it from a certain salty death. It contained all of the digital photos we had taken throughout our safari. If we had lost it we would have been inconsolable! We didn't have time to be relieved because we were tipping once again. We hung on and leaned into the centerline of the boat, hoping our little efforts might help! After quite a dashing ride the wind stopped, the sail hung slack, and we were floating along with just a gentle bobbing of the dhow. Other dhows were resting in the same spot and they, too, were simply floating. One nearby was a party boat. The guests were happily diving into the water for a swim. We enjoyed watching them swim, but none of us had the desire to leave our dhow!

The sunset was delicious, and so was the wine that the first mate arrived with and, joining us on the platform, poured for us. Ahh, windswept and sun kissed, our spirits soared as if we were sitting on top of the world! Once the sun had set and the sky darkened, the crew prepared for our trip home. For some reason, whether we had acquired sea fannies or the wine gave us the courage, we managed the entire ride home on top of the platform.

Our final challenge was departing from the boat. The water had risen because the tide was swiftly coming in, which also meant we had farther to go. To add to the adventure, both the water and the sky were now pitch black. There was nothing to do but go down the ladder and over the side. We slid into the cool water while holding our belongings above our heads. Martin, who was safeguarding the camera, wasn't able to hold on to me at the same time. I surged forward; Charlotte stumbled and cried out to Chris. He was right behind her and soon had his arms around her. I kept my eye on Martin, concerned for the irreplaceable photos of our trip. I felt queasy from being in water over my shoulders. The four of us headed toward the lights on land. I truly hoped that nothing aquatic would bump into any of us before we reached the beach. We all made it ashore without losing any gear and with great relief we gave each other huge, wet bear hugs! It is amazing how close you can get to two other people when you have shared an adventure on the high seas! In less than an hour we were dressed for dinner and, in the lobby's comfy couches, learning how to play a variation of mancala with our new friends from London.

Monkey Drama!

Tuesday, October 23

We woke up to a gorgeous morning, only a single menacing cloud marred the sky before slipping by without dampening our day. We ate our usual delectable breakfast and prepared for our next adventure, a trip to the Jozani Forest to capture photos of the rare red colobus monkey. The trip was a long two-hour ride through the central part of Zanzibar. Being mostly flat and dry, it was nowhere nearly as glorious as the turquoise waters of the coast. Once we arrived at the park and signed in to the guest register, our guide promptly greeted us and introduced herself as Mdonna. I enthusiastically stated that my name was Donna,

Rare red colobus monkey

too, but I was corrected immediately; she pronounced her name again this time emphasizing the *m* sound as, *mmmmdonna*. With her hair and neck covered in a bright yellow veil, she resembled a freshly sprouted daffodil. She wore a matching long-sleeved, yellow blouse with a narrow, long, green skirt that tickled the tops of her sandals. It was a hot day, well into the nineties! I wondered if she was steaming inside all of that clothing. She was crisp, to the point, and very professional. However, she informed us that it was a "Hot, too-hot day!" That simple statement answered the question I had wished to ask since we arrived in Zanzibar but hadn't, in case it would be considered rude. It *was* hot for the women with the many layers of clothing and head coverings.

We were soon to learn that Mdonna was a walking encyclopedia of nature as we followed her from the main camp area down a dirt road to the beginnings of the forest. It cooled down under the shade of the tall canopy of trees. Mdonna pointed out a monkey chomping on a leaf. He looked at us with the interest of a disapproving old woman! He finished his leaf and briskly turned his back on us; his fur shone the same reddish-burnt sienna color as the soil above the Ngorongoro Crater.

We ventured farther into the forest, craning our necks to watch networks of monkeys jumping from branch to branch and cavorting above our heads. Mdonna made a point to tell us, "Beware of monkey rain. They often pee on their visitors!"

We tucked into a burrow of trees alive with monkeys. I quickly realized a drama was taking place. A baby monkey was plaintively screeching! An adult monkey was holding onto the little one and picking insects off it, much to the infant's displeasure. I thought for a moment that it was just a child protesting an unwanted cleaning. But, more drama unfolded; we watched as another monkey approached and grabbed hold of the legs of the baby. The baby screamed pitifully. The two adults held tight to the poor monkey at either end. I was afraid the little thing would rip into two! I wondered if we were witnessing a "monkey-napping"? The approaching monkey, however, was more aggressive and with one great yank retrieved the baby from the other adult. The victor proved to be the rightful mother, because as soon as she freed the baby from her captor she gently calmed its whimpers by breast-feeding her little one. The wrongful adult squawked threateningly at them; then, giving up, she hopped to another tree and out of sight.

We asked Mdonna if it was indeed a monkey-napping by an auntie who didn't have a baby to fuss over. She nodded and answered, "Yes, she would like to have a baby of her own, so she tried to take the baby from the mother!"

We continued on the path through mangroves and over a bridge to another area of the park. The trees seemed ancient and regal; Mdonna informed us that this was the oldest part of the forest. Sunlight streamed through the leaves and birds chirped and twittered at us dreamily. Finishing up our tour of the park, we parted with a final *asante sana* and climbed into our waiting vehicle.

Upon arrival back at paradise, we said, "*Asante sana*," to our driver and gave him his expected, but folded, tip. We felt quite happy to stretch our legs. We strolled leisurely to our seaside abode and decided to luxuriate on our last afternoon by taking a swim and going for a walk on the beach. We had just entered our hut when we heard a sharp knock. We found an excited bellhop outside our door. He relayed that a man from the village had come with a package and was waiting for us in the reception area. We scurried to reception

Dhow delivered

to find our boat builder from the day before holding a wooden box. Martin greeted him by shaking his hand, and he smiled back with a huge smile. He opened the box to show us the completed dhow, with masts sewn and all the details intact. It smelled of fresh varnish and appeared to be slightly tacky. It was a magnificent piece of work! Martin was beaming and paid him his asked-for price of fifty dollars, along with an additional tip for finishing so quickly. His smile grew even larger, and then he said, "Thank you," in English. He spoke the words perfectly. He had fooled both Roger and us! We laughed feeling slightly embarrassed that he understood the entire two-way conversation that took place on the beach the day before. We took pictures of him, Martin, and the dhow, and he gave us his email address.

We took our new treasure back to our room and aired it out as much as we could before it had to be boxed up again. It dried out well and made it home without a problem. Of course, Martin hand-carried the wooden box the whole way home. It is now proudly displayed, with its mast in full sail, in our living room.

It was our last afternoon and the sun was beginning to sink in the western sky. In an effort to hold onto our paradise home Martin took some final photographs of Nungwi. One of our favorite photos was of the women walking barefoot down the beach, with their long skirts and scarves flowing, carrying huge piles of sticks on their heads for firewood. This was their life, a daily rhythm required for the cooking of dinner that evening. They paced this chore with long, steady strides, unhurried and flowing like the waves of the Indian Ocean.

That evening, before our dinner, we learned how to play the most difficult form of mancala, an African marble game. It kept our brains turning full tilt with the strategy and cleverness of the ancient game. We dined under the stars and slept well afterward, dreaming of the next day's trip to Stonetown.

Women walking on the beach

Daily chore

THE SPICE ISLAND

Wednesday, October 24

After giving a full round of folded tips to all our waiters and bellhops, we said a sad *asante sana* and *kwaheri* to Ras Nungwi Resort. Waiting for us in reception, we met our new driver who would transport us to Stonetown.

We stopped along the way for a spice-farm tour. I learned why Zanzibar is called the spice island. We saw ginger, vanilla beans, nutmeg, lemongrass, cloves, cinnamon bark, cayenne, and teas of all kinds—more than I can name. We learned that there are spice farms in abundance in Zanzibar; Arabs who settled in Zanzibar long ago brought the spice seeds and plants to the island. After a tour of the gardens and grounds, our tour guide led us to a gigantic coconut tree. "*Jambo, jambo*!" A young man with a rope tied taut around his ankles greeted us; then he proceeded to ascend the tree. He sang as he climbed. When he reached midway, he swung his feet outward from the tree! We gasped as he lifted his body with only the strength of his arms to a ninety-degree angle from the tree. The muscles on his arms were bulging! And all the while he sang the song, "*Jambo, jambo*!" After this spectacular display, he realigned himself to the coconut tree and continued to climb to the top where the coconuts were ripe. Hanging on by his knees he cut a coconut with one swift slice of his knife and soon was on his way back down, using only one hand and his roped feet. Ouch! My ankles groaned in sympathy! If we were to try this, we wouldn't make it more than a foot above the ground and our skin would rip off from the rasp and burn of the rope. Upon his return to earth, we gave him a resounding round of applause. He cut open the coconut and gave us each a refreshing drink! We said, "*Asante sana*," and of course Martin, with folded bills, handed him a tip.

Our guide had more in store for our entertainment. He magically created crowns for us out of palm fronds. In seconds he wove a tie for Martin and a bracelet for me, but the best fun was the palm leaf sunglasses!

We purchased tons of spices, soap, teas, and perfumes. With bags filled to the brim we said, "*Asante sana*," to our guide. We were ready for Stonetown.

Donna's new sunglasses

Serena Hotel, Stonetown

Indian Ocean. Thomson Safaris planned our trip extremely well: from sleeping in tents, to a charming coffee plantation cottage, to the delightful amenities of Ras Nungwi, culminating with the ultimate luxury of the Serena Hotel!

The hammock on the balcony beckoned me. But so did the luxurious oversized wooden chairs with plump pillows where we could watch the dhows with full sails float by. Then we saw bathers swimming in the enormous pool below our balcony where fountain sculptures of white fish gurgled a steady stream of clear water into the pool. The temperature had risen to mid-ninety; feeling limp and travel weary, we were ready to be refreshed. We quickly donned our bathing suits and a full cover up for me; then we grabbed some beach towels and headed for the cool, refreshing waters.

On our way down the steps to the pool I was surprised to see an armed guard on duty. He was stationed where the hotel grounds ended and the long and very wide public beach met. We had been warned by our greeter, and by signs placed throughout the hotel, not to go on the beach or anywhere alone after dark, and to take care on the beach during the day! They, the greeter and the signs, didn't say what could happen to us if we didn't obey, but my imagination filled in the blanks. Martin and I decided it was best to be wise and listen to their advice. But, inside, we felt safe and could

Stonetown! What a contrast it was coming from the relaxing atmosphere of Ras Nungwi to see people zipping in and out of the traffic on bikes, motorcycles revving their engines, cars lined up bumper to bumper, trucks loaded with produce, and buses filled to the brim with riders and their market purchases. People walked every which way. It was a dense mob scene exploding in front of our eyes. Our savvy driver knew how to maneuver us through the thickest of the commotion, landing us expertly in front of our destination: the regal and very Arabic looking Serena Hotel. We were greeted warmly by an extremely tall man clad in a long, flowing, white robe and turban. We were ushered up to the second floor and graciously led to an elegant room with a view. It had a large corner balcony facing the

Our balcony

suits and rested on our balcony, where we could easily have spent the entire evening. Between the soccer game of sorts being played on the beach, the constant flow of dhows going past, and the golden sun beginning its decent into the Indian Ocean, we couldn't have asked for more.

Martin donned his dress shirt, tie, and nice slacks, while I wore my best skirt and blouse combo; luckily our laundry was holding out from hand washing! After changing, we wandered through the hotel, soaking up the beauty that emanated from every hallway and corner. The hotel itself was made up of two buildings, with the pool connecting the two parts. On the far side, there was a lovely outdoor café and terrace. To our

enjoy every amenity that this handsome Arabic hotel provided. After a delicious swim we stretched out on the chaise lounges with thick, decadent cushions. Life surely couldn't get better than this, but then it did! We were served sugared crepes made on the terrace of the pool to be washed down with mugs of freshly steeped Zanzibar tea.

We liked the look of the restaurant near the pool, but the crepe chef informed us that there was a very special dining room on the top of the roof. That sounded romantic and since it was our only night in Stonetown, we made a reservation. We changed out of our bathing

delight, an all-female band was performing. They were completely covered in long purple dresses, with shawls, scarves, and head coverings. They sang in English, but the sound was very Middle Eastern, most likely because Zanzibar is 90% Muslim. Several of the women sang solos and all of the ladies played an instrument. Soon the sky darkened and our reservation for dinner was calling us. We followed the signs to the top of the building. It was a hike up quite a narrow staircase, not what you would expect to be the route to a romantic, rooftop restaurant! As we climbed I contemplated the meaning of the sign in the lobby that said "Do not go

Dhow at sunset

A lovely rooftop dinner

out alone at night." I wondered, did it mean don't go out as a woman alone? Or did it mean alone, as a couple, or a group without a guide? Should I interpret it as a safety warning for all tourists, or did they simply want to keep their own guests inside? I was thankful we were dining inside the hotel!

When we reached the top, we were seated at a table for two on the ocean side with nothing but stars and sky above us. The restaurant was distinctly romantic with twinkling lights and the warm glow of candles. The servers were in white robes and turbans that matched the crisp white tablecloths and napkins. I ordered lobster and was served three! Our waiter was especially friendly. He had a great sense of humor, entertaining us as he served us a most delicious and memorable meal.

Stonetown

Thursday, October 25

We woke up to a very warm and sunny day in the high 80s. The dhows sailed past with masts billowing in the early morning, sparkling, turquoise water. After a full breakfast, served buffet style, we were ready for our tour of Stonetown. Our guide showed up, a young man dressed in sandals, jeans, T-shirt, and a warm smile. We followed him as he led us into the labyrinth of streets. We were glad to have a guide, and quite a happy one! The wider roads soon narrowed into a maze of intersecting lines that became streets for foot traffic. People were everywhere. Doors were thrown open to reveal dwellings with six, eight, or twelve people huddled around a fire eating a mid-morning meal. Chickens ran free with the children, who played in the middle of the streets. Motorbikes would suddenly appear and everyone would scatter as they *vroomed* by. We passed many small shops with doors wide open and merchandise literally spilling out onto the street. The merchants in the midst of their wares beckoned us to enter: "*Karibu*! *Karibu*!"

In the center of these passageways ran a river of water. I didn't want to think of what, besides water, it might contain, and I regretted wearing open-toe sandals. The streets were alive, bustling with energy and activity. We followed in a straight line like chicks behind our new mother hen. Our guide kept his eye on us and told us not to wander from him. We did not wish to buy anything at this point in our trip, which worked out fine, because he warned us not to do any shopping. If we wanted to look we should peek in from outside because, if we entered, the shopkeepers would make sure we would not leave without buying something!

Stonetown, Zanzibar

Two women shopping

outside the home. He said that they can come and go and no one knows who it is behind the veil. I have my doubts about the truth of that statement. To me it seemed horrendously unfair that men can wear jeans and short-sleeved shirts with bare arms and heads and women have to completely cover themselves.

Two women, dressed in full burqas, passed us on the street. I could tell they were young by the way their robes fit, defining feminine silhouettes. Our guide spoke to them in a friendly manner. I asked, "Do you know them, or are you flirting with them?"

He answered, "What is this floating you are talking about?"

I laughed and said, "Not floating, flirting! It is when you talk nice to the girls because you like them."

He quickly answered, "Oh, yes, I like girls very much!"

I sensed the girls liked the attention; you could see their eyes smiling and one stopped to adjust her skirt giving a quick glimpse of sandaled foot and ankle!

Hot and hungry, we returned to the hotel. We thanked our guide and Martin gave him some folded bills. We then had a quick lunch and had time to pack before our ride to the airport arrived. We said *asante sana* and *kwaheri* to the beautiful Serena Hotel as we contemplated our long trip back home.

He led us to where slaves had once been auctioned off, heart-breaking pages of history, thankfully in the distant past. We then moved on to the marketplace, teaming with people and their wares. Carts spilled over with aromatic teas and spices. Women dressed in full burqas were busy shopping. Some of the robes the women wore were intricately embroidered and elaborately designed. These women were not without a sense of fashion! Our guide told us that they do not mind wearing the burqa even though many husbands no longer require that they wear them. Many women choose to wear them to give them privacy when appearing

Young woman in full burqa

Our driver brought us directly to the airport and upon entering we were met by many long lines; it was confusing to say the least. There was no attendant available to ask which line we needed to be in. Once we got our bearings, we located the right line and waited to check in. Our names were found on a list and checked off. We had to check our duffle bags and we were seriously concerned that all our treasures wouldn't make it onto the correct plane. The waiting room was small and packed to the hilt with passengers. We luckily found two empty seats. There was much drama and a lot of commotion. We watched dismayed people discovering that their names were not on the list for the flight they anticipated being on. Eventually a young man called out our flight number and proceeded to lead our group to a small airplane. We climbed into the plane, found two seats, and tightened our seat belts. It turned out to be a bumpy flight over the Indian Ocean. I took a deep breath as we headed for Dar es Salaam.

On our arrival at Dar es Salaam, we thankfully grabbed our two duffle bags and exited into the general pick up area. Our new driver, as had all the others, found us as if we were carrying a huge neon sign blaring our names. He ushered us to a car and told us that he would drive us to a hotel in town where we could take a shower, repack if necessary, and have a good meal. Our itinerary listed the ride as a short fifteen minutes away, but it turned into its own adventure! To say that Dar es Salaam was teaming with people would be a serious understatement. There were bumper-to-bumper cars for miles on both sides of the road. Young men with tall plastic buckets on their heads walked easily between the cars selling cans of soda. It was like a street festival. You could buy a CD of local African music from more than one passing moveable merchant or a bag of fresh nuts to go with your soda!

After more than an hour-long ride, we arrived at the hotel where we were efficiently checked in and shown our room. How luxurious to be relaxing in a lovely hotel instead of sitting in an airport all afternoon and early evening! We were continually amazed at how all our arrivals and departures in Africa were so smoothly prearranged by Thomson Safaris in Watertown, Massachusetts. We were constantly cared for and never left stranded without a guide. Well aware of the fact that we had a long night of travel ahead, we took our showers and stretched out on the bed for a short nap. Feeling refreshed, we wandered down to the restaurant. It seemed nice and had a good menu. As we were seated at a cozy table my stomach rumbled, lunch had been eons away.

We were picked up at eight o'clock sharp for our eleven o'clock flight. Our newest driver was very helpful getting our knapsacks and duffle bags into the car. We hopped in and began our hour-and-a-half journey to the airport. If we thought the traffic was bad going into town, it was worse going out. The major difference was that this time it was dark. We had nothing to do but wait it out. When we arrived back at the Dar es Salaam airport, our driver parked the car, hopped out, and said, "Wait here." Without any other explanation, he mysteriously headed in the opposite direction of the airport. We watched till he was no longer visible, wondering *where did he go?* We got out of the car and stood there pondering what to do. There were porters everywhere piling up people's luggage and escorting them to the check-in stations. Martin opened the trunk and pulled out our duffles. We were soon approached by a porter who was glad to take all our bags and us to the check in. We took one last look, and seeing no sign of our driver, we said yes to the porter and off we went. Our driver did not get his tip, and we never did figure out what happened to him, or why he left us in such a hurry.

We flew KLM to Amsterdam. We had saved up our points and were lucky to fly business class, which provided fully reclining chairs. I was able to grab a little sleep on our nine-hour flight but Martin didn't sleep a wink. After a four-hour wait in Amsterdam, we boarded our Delta flight for the seven-hour flight home to Boston. All I remember was that the last part of the flight was a bit bumpy, waking me every few minutes. The rest was a blur of half dreams about cheetahs cavorting, striped zebras standing at attention in long lines, Maasai children carrying babies sling-style on their backs, young warriors running through the bush, lions sleeping with paws in the air, coffee plantations full of purple jacaranda flowers, silly warthogs scratching, balloon rides over the Serengeti, sailing in dhows on the Indian Ocean with full masts, the golden glow of waking up in a tent, elephants showering dust on themselves, Muslim school children counting with their fingers, cinnamon-chested bee-eaters buzzing, wildebeests snorting all night long, and bumpy rides in the Range Rover with Kileo calling to us, "Just hold on!"

Vast Serengeti plains

Donna under the African sky

Home!

Friday, October 26

We were at last home, tired, but happy, from an incredible trip of a lifetime! I will never forget the feeling of how small I felt under the never-ending African sky, the immense vastness of the Serengeti plains, and the absolute majesty of the beasts along with the richness of the African people.

Asante sana, Tanzania! *Asante sana,* Thomson Safaris!

Swahili, the Official Language of Tanzania

Donna's Vocabulary list

Pronunciation guide

Vowels: a = ah, e = eh, i = ee, o = oh, u = oo
Consonants are pronounced as in English.

Pleasantries

Jambo, Jambo (Jahm-boh): Hello, Greetings!
Habari? (Hah-bahr-ee): How are you?
Mzuri, asante sana (Ma-zoor-ee) (Ah-sahn-teh sah-nah): Good (I am well), thank you very much.
Tafadhali (Tah-fah-dhahl-ee): Please, (a very important word to use often!)
Asante (Ah-sahn-teh): Thank you
Sana (Sah nah): Very much
Asante sana (Ah-sahn-teh sah-nah): Thank you very much, (important to always say!)
Karibu (Kah-ree-boo): Welcome!
Lala salama (Lah-lah sah-lahm-ah): Sleep well, (If you repeat this, you will fall asleep!)
Kwaheri (Kwah-heh-ree): Goodbye
Twende (Twehn-deh): Let's go!

Safari nouns

Rafiki (Rah-fee-kee): Friend
Tembo (Tehm-boh): Elephant
Simba (Seem-bah): Lion
Chui (Choo-ee): Leopard
Duma (Doom-ah): Cheetah
Twiga (Tweeg-ah): Giraffe
Nyumbu (Ny-oom-boo): Wildebeest
Swala (Swah-lah): Gazelle
Punda millia (Poon dah meel lee ah): Zebra (Punda = donkey, millia = stripes)
Punda (Poon-dah): Donkey (zebra without millia, or stripes!)

Food and drink

Chai (Chah-ee): tea
Chai tafadhali (Chah-ee tah-fah-dhahl-ee): Tea, please
Kuku (Koo-koo): Chicken
Maji (Mah-jee): Water
Supu (soo-poo): Soup
Pombe (Pohm-beh) Beer
Kwa afya! (Kwah ahf-yah) Cheers!

Fun facts about Africa

These facts were garnered from what we learned on our safari, our fact-filled *Thomson safari journal*, our many guides and drivers on safari, and online with African Travel Expert, Anouk Ziflma.

- At birth a baby giraffe drops six feet to the ground, and within a mere five minutes it's standing up.
- A giraffe's tongue is dark blue and extends up to twenty inches to retrieve the tastiest new growth at the tops of the trees.
- The cheetah is the fastest land animal on earth, covering up to thirty feet in one leap.
- The cheetah can reach seventy miles an hour before you can snap your fingers.
- Elephants, hippos, and rhinos are all vegetarians!
- If a hippo yawns at you, you are in big trouble.
- Hippos eat a hefty 100 pounds of grass and plants a day.
- Hippos poop sixty pounds a day, and when they do they spin their tails!
- Elephants speak to each other with rumbles and grumbles.
- Baby elephants suck on their trunks just like a baby sucking its thumb.
- Elephant dung looks like small bales of hay. If you burn it and breathe in the smoke it will cure a migraine headache.
- When swimming, elephants use their trunks as a snorkel.
- A lion can sleep twenty hours a day!
- Lions, like domestic cats, do not like to swim.
- Crocodiles and their ancestors date back 200 million years.
- Only big crocs will attack a full grown human, little crocs will just bite your finger off. No petting big or little crocs!
- A group of rhinos is called a *crash*.
- Rhinos are shortsighted and short-tempered.
- There are black rhinos and white rhinos, but both are grey. The only difference is their lips.
- A rhino horn is made of keratin, the same as a horse's hoof. No magical medicine included.
- There are no two zebras alike! Every zebra has its own unique set of stripes—like our fingerprints.
- At dusk and dawn, the zebra's stripes blend together into a perfect camouflage!
- The dung beetle rolls up animal dung into a neat little ball, lays its eggs in it, and buries it. Great clean-up crew!
- During the Great Migration every year, wildebeests give birth to 90% of their offspring in the month of February, all on the same southern Serengeti plain.
- The Great Migration is the yearly, five-hundred-mile journey, of one and a half million wildebeests, zebras, and gazelles through the Serengeti and bordering lands, seeking better grazing and water. This incredible phenomenon is the largest wildlife movement on earth!

Thompson gazelle (tommy)

Author, Donna Marie Seim and Photographer, Martin Seim

Donna is the award-winning author of two children's picture books and two middle grade readers.

Where is Simon, Sandy? is set on the island of Grand Turk. It is the story of a little donkey that wouldn't quit.

Satchi and Little Star is the story of an island girl who tries to catch and tame a wild horse.

Hurricane Mia is an adventure story of a young girl who sets out to find the tea that cures everything.

Charley, set in 1910, is based on a true story of a streetwise city boy from Boston who, after being abandoned, finds himself taken in by a dairy farming family in rural Maine.

Martin, photographer extraordinaire, has practiced the art of photography since the age of seven, when he received his first Brownie camera.

Maasai family patriarch